Touring Tennessee

Touring Tennessee

a postcard panorama

1898-1955

Ridley Wills II

HILLSBORO PRESS
Franklin, Tennessee

TENNESSEE HERITAGE LIBRARY
Bicentennial Collection

Printed in the United States of America

00   99   98   97   96   1   2   3   4   5

Library of Congress Catalog Card Number: 96–78433

ISBN: 1–881576–98–1

Cover by Susan Hulme

Published by
HILLSBORO PRESS
an imprint of
PROVIDENCE HOUSE PUBLISHERS
238 Seaboard Lane • Franklin, Tennessee 37067
800-321-5692

TO MY SONS

Ridley III, Jesse, Morgan, and Tom.

Although Jesse did not live long
enough to fully comprehend how much
I loved him, my other sons know that
they are, and always have been, a joy to
their mother and me.

Contents

*F*oreword

TOURING TENNESSEE: A POSTCARD HISTORY 1898-1955 is a fascinating look at Tennessee history during the first half of the twentieth century, as documented by local historian Ridley Wills II. Over the last three decades, Wills has amassed a superb collection of Tennessee postcards, totaling nearly thirteen thousand different images of people, places, and events that have been part of the Tennessee experience. The collection includes images from towns and cities, from farms and factories, from schools and universities, from churches and businesses, and from black and white Tennesseans. This book not only represents a cross section of the collection, but it also reveals the duel quality of the postcard as a historical source. On the one hand, most postcards served merely as advertisements for the sponsoring business, industry, or tourist destination; they often were nothing more than a booster for a local chamber of commerce or civic group. Thus, these cards offer important insight on the nature of promotion, advertisement, and commercial design in the early twentieth century. On the other hand, postcards offer significant documentary evidence about city streets, individual buildings, and larger landscapes that no longer exist in Tennessee. In fact, what struck me most forcibly about this book is how many of the

places are now part of a lost Tennessee. I can remember the sad demolition of the James K. Polk Hotel in Murfreesboro during the mid-1970s. But what happened to the Sampson Sanitarium in Smith County or the Sedberry Hotel in Warren County? These buildings are now gone, but fortunately, they are not entirely "lost" because these postcards record their appearance and activities. Future generations of historians, historic preservationists, and students of historic architecture will benefit from a careful study of these different postcards.

In the first half of this century, postcards allowed travelers to send their memories of a place to family and friends back home. Now these same cards will allow us to recreate, if only in part, the sense of place and memory that characterized early-twentieth-century Tennessee. Especially at the time of the Tennessee Bicentennial, Ridley Wills should be congratulated for bringing this collection, and the many messages it conveys, to our attention.

Carroll Van West
Senior Editor, *Tennessee Historical Quarterly*
Center for Historic Preservation
Middle Tennessee State University

Introduction

In 1961 I moved back to Nashville after working for two years in Georgia and Ohio as a salesman for the National Life and Accident Insurance Company. Some time after returning home, I took a camera downtown to take photographs of some old buildings I was interested in. I specifically remember standing on Fourth Avenue North between Commerce and Church Streets taking a picture of the Cumberland Presbyterian Building. Two problems came to mind. One was a reservation about my ability as a photographer. The more serious one was that so many of the buildings I wanted pictures of were gone. As a matter of fact, as I stood there the Cumberland Presbyterian Building was being demolished. This led me to consider another method of recapturing "Old Nashville." I decided to look in the closet of my bedroom in my parents' home to see if any postcards were left from my boyhood collection. There, in a shoe box, I found what I was looking for—a few postcards, most of which were of the linen variety, published from 1930

Fig. 1. William H. Taft, Horace H. Lurton, and Jacob M. Dickinson at Belle Meade, May 21, 1908.

to 1944. One postcard that particularly caught my eye showed William Howard Taft, Judge H. H. Lurton, and Jacob McGavock Dickinson (fig. 1) seated in front of the breezeway at the Belle Meade Stock Farm near Nashville. The picture was much older than the others. A little investigation revealed that it was published soon after Taft, then secretary of war, visited Nashville in May 1908 to address the twenty-fifth annual convention of the Tennessee Bar Association. Jacob McGavock Dickinson, a future secretary of war, who owned Belle Meade, hosted a barbecue for Mr. Taft, his houseguest. After the barbecue, Taft, Dickinson, and Horace H. Lurton, a former chief justice of the Tennessee Supreme Court and future associate justice on the United States Supreme Court, posed for the picture.

I thought the Belle Meade postcard was marvelous and wondered if enough old Nashville postcards were still available to satisfy my interest. I quickly began to collect Nashville postcards, consciously trying to find ones I remembered from my childhood collection. Little did I suspect that from that modest start I would build a collection that would total

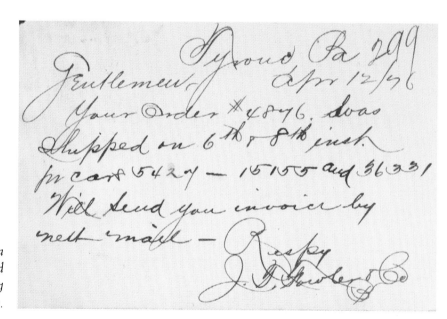

Fig. 2. This image is of the backside of a postal card, dated April 12, 1876. The card was addressed to the American Dredging Company in Philadelphia.

Fig. 3. This postal card was mailed from Baltimore February 21, 1881, by a salesman asking for instructions from his employer.

more than 12,800 Tennessee postcards in 1996—including 2,200 from Nashville. Where in the world, you might ask, did I find so many postcards? The answer is *everywhere.* One dependable source was from dealers at the monthly flea market held at the Tennessee State Fairgrounds in Nashville. There, I have purchased hundreds of postcards from Ray Pelley of Paducah, Kentucky, a collector and antique dealer who brought his postcards to the Nashville flea market each month for many years. Even before I met Ray, I traded and bought postcards from Edward L. Bruce, a Nashville collector.

Antique stores and flea markets have been especially good sources for me. I have looked for postcards in every antique store in Nashville and in antique stores and flea markets across the country. My wife, who is an antique collector, long ago found that I was perfectly content for her to spend time in antique stores as I pursued my considerably less-expensive search for postcards. I must say that the higher the scale of the antique store the less the probability that I would be successful. A rule of thumb I've learned is that the farther you are from your own state the

Fig. 4. This equestrian statue by Clark Mills was erected on May 20, 1880, the one hundredth anniversary of Nashville's founding.

Fig. 5. Only the address could be written on this side of the Private Mailing Card. (See figure 4 for front view.)

3

Copyright 1905 by the Rotograph Co.
® 14547 Front Street, Memphis, Tenn.

This is my first visit to the South & I am delighted

Fig. 6. Memphis's Cossitt Library is the red brick building with a tower on the left. Behind it is the larger Custom House.

POST CARD

The Rotograph Co., N. Y. City. (Germany.)

This side for the Address.

Mrs. Ida Clay.
Parker's Landing.
Armstrong Co.,
Penna

Fig. 7. This postcard was postmarked twice—once in Memphis where it was mailed and again in Parker's Landing, Pennsylvania, where it was received. (See figure 6 for front view.)

less expensive postcards from your area are likely to be.

Periodically, I have attended postcard trade shows in Nashville and the Mid-south. Often, you can get discounts of 10 to 20 percent from postcard and antique dealers if you buy more than a minimum amount. To find out the names and addresses of postcard dealers in your area, I suggest you write the International Federation of Postcard Dealers, P. O. Box 1765, Manassas, Virginia 22110.

Earlier in my collecting years, I subscribed to *Barr's Post Card News*, a weekly periodical published at 70 South Sixth Street, Lansing, Iowa, 52151. *Barr's* features pictures of postcards available for sale and their estimated auction values. Another such periodical is the *Post Card Collector*, P. O. Box 1050, Dubuque, Iowa 52004-1050. I never had much luck in purchasing postcards from these sources because they were usually expensive. A more productive method of enhancing my collection has been to trade postcards with other private collectors whose interests have been similar. Over time, as acquaintances have become aware of my postcard hobby,

Fig. 8. The bodies of John J. Andrews and seven fellow raiders were interred in Chattanooga's National Cemetery on October 16, 1887. The Union soldiers were executed as spies, following their capture after a chase on the Western & Atlantic Railroad in April 1862. A miniature replica of the engine they captured, the General, is on top of the monument.

Fig. 9. The U.S. Postal Service delivered this postcard (mailed in Estill Springs on June 28, 1907) in one day to Lawrenceburg.

they have called to tell me about the existence of postcards that might be of interest to me. Also, estate sales occasionally provide opportunities to buy inexpensively entire collections of postcards of little interest to heirs.

As my postcard collection grew, the history of postcards became more interesting to me. I found that the Austrian government first introduced postcards in 1869. England, Germany, and Switzerland began issuing post-cards the next year. Soon, other European countries and Canada followed suit. The first postcard introduced in the United States was on July 1, 1872. The United States Post Office established a one-cent postal-card rate, anticipating that the postal cards would be used for "orders, invitations, notices, receipts, acknowledgments, price lists, and other requirements of business and social life, according to Gary L. Dostor, editor of *From Abbeville to Zebulon: Early Post Card Views of Georgia*. Figures 2 and 3 are of two early United States postal cards, both used for business purposes.

The first picture postcards available for public use were printed by a Paris newspaper for the Exposition Universelle in Paris in 1889. The

"Echo Valley Retreat" for Tourists.   Mrs. W. E. Youree, Hostess, Readyville, Tennessee

Fig. 10. Readyville, a small community on the Cannon-Rutherford county line, was named for Charles Ready, who settled there in 1802. Ready's great-granddaughter, Martha "Mattie" Ready, married Brig. Gen. John Hunt Morgan, Confederate States of America.

Fig. 11. Nashville's Christ Episcopal Church is on the left side of Broadway, across Ninth Avenue North from the five-story Methodist Publishing House.

postcards, which included pictures of the Eiffel Tower completed earlier that year, were sold at the base of the tower as souvenirs. Four years later, picture postcards were sold for the first time in the United States—as souvenirs of the World Columbian Exposition in Chicago. These cards were so popular that Congress passed legislation on May 19, 1898, allowing private printing companies to publish and sell picture postcards that could be mailed for a one-cent postage stamp provided they were marked "Private Mailing Card" on the back. The backside of the card was used exclusively for the name and address. The other side, or front, had a picture with a space below it or to the side on which a short message could be written. This era lasted three years. Figures 4 and 5 show both sides of a Private Mailing Card featuring a picture of Gen. Andrew Jackson's statue on the State Capitol grounds in Nashville.

Beginning December 24, 1901, the U.S. Post Office permitted the use of the words "Post Card" on the back or address side of the card, but still only the name and address was allowed on that side. This period is called the "undivided back postcard" era because there was no dividing line on the address side of the card. The front side with the picture still had a narrow space for the message. The "undivided back" era lasted from late 1901 until March 1,1907. Figures 6 and 7 show both sides of an undivided back postcard of Front Street in Memphis.

Beginning March 1, 1907, postcards with a divided back were permitted. The picture on the front side could then cover the entire space. The message was written on the back, with the address to the right and the message to the left. Shown in figures 8 and 9 are both sides of an early divided-back postcard of the Andrews Raiders Monument in Chattanooga's National Cemetery.

The divided-back postcard marked the start of the enormous popularity of picture postcards in the United States. Not only were they mailed to show the folks back home scenes of cities and towns that people had visited, but postcard collecting became extremely popular. The name "deltiology" was coined to give a name to the craze of postcard collecting.

The next era in postcards began in 1915 when postcards were printed with white borders. This period, characterized by inferior postcards, lasted until 1930. However, some postcards were produced without white borders until 1920, which makes dating them somewhat confusing. Shown in figure 10 is a white-bordered postcard of an early tourist home in Readyville, Tennessee.

On November 3, 1917, the U.S. Postal Service increased the postage for picture postcards from one to two cents. On July 1, 1919, this

Fig. 12. Tracy City.

Fig 13. Chattanooga.

postage increase was rescinded. In 1925, the rate again went to two cents and stayed at that amount until August 1, 1958, when it increased to three cents. Since then, increases have been more frequent. The rate jumped to four cents on January 7, 1963, to five cents five years later, and to six cents on May 16, 1971. Since then there have been numerous increases with the current rate being twenty cents.

At one time, I became interested in who published the postcards in my collection. I found that during the golden years of postcard collecting in the United States, which was roughly between 1905 and 1915, many were published locally—often by the town drugstore where postcards were usually sold. They could also be found at book stores, hotels, and railroad stations. Many of the first postcards were published by one of several national publishers, including the Rotograph Company of New York City, E. C. Kropp Company of Milwaukee, and S. H. Kress & Company. Clearly, most postcards published between 1901 and 1914 were printed in Europe. Thousands were produced by Raphael Tuck & Sons, which reported to be "art publishers to their majesties the King and Queen" of England on the back of its cards. Most, however, were color lithographs published in Germany, where printing companies had better equipment than did their American competitors.

Curt Teich of Chicago was another major domestic player in producing postcards of American scenes. The Curt Teich Postcard Archives at the Lake County Museum, Lakewood Forest Preserve, Wauconda, Illinois 60084, has a permanent exhibition of postcards published by

Curt Teich. It also has a reproduction service through which you can order photographic prints or transparencies of any postcards in the collection. The telephone number in 1996 was (847) 526-8638. In recent years, Debra Gust, a researcher there, has been very helpful to me in obtaining color copies of Tennessee postcards I did not have in my collection.

Some of the postcards from the early 1900s were printed in black and white, while others, also printed in black and white, were hand-colored. Figure 11 is of a postcard of the latter type. It shows a bird's-eye view of downtown Nashville, including Christ Episcopal Church at the southwest corner of Ninth and Broadway. The artist, who hand colored the card, painted Christ Episcopal Church red. As the building was built of Sewanee Mountain sandstone, it should have been a light gray color. Notice the absence of the church tower. It would not be completed until 1947.

Early in the twentieth century, novelty cards were produced by the thousands. Three are shown in figures 12, 13, and 14. Figure 13 of a couple in a swing in Chattanooga, postmarked in 1911, was similar to romantic postcards published for all of the country's larger cities. In that sense it could also be categorized as a generic postcard. The postcard in figure 14 shows the east end of the Parthenon in Nashville. The large building in the background with the flag above it was the Commerce Building at the Tennessee Centennial Celebration. The postcard features tiny colored particles that glitter.

Postcard collecting became less popular during World War I when access to the good German printers was cut off and when travel in the United States was severely curtailed. Following the war, the increased popularity of telephones and automobiles were other factors that caused postcards to lose some of their appeal. When people could stay in touch by telephone, there was less reason to send messages by postcard. As roads improved and automobile travel became more popular, people became more mobile and the need to communicate by postcard became less important. However, postcards continued to be produced.

1986 The Parthenon, Centennial Park, Nashville, Tenn.

Fig. 14. Parthenon, Nashville.

9

The linen-postcard era began in 1930. They were produced through World War II. Figure 15 shows a linen card of Howard's Manor and Cottages in Millington, Tennessee, eighteen miles north of Memphis. During the 1950s, the motel featured innerspring mattresses and tile baths in every room. To phone for a reservation, you were instructed to dial 170-Millington.

In 1945, the photochrome era of postcards began. "Chrome" cards were first produced by the Union Oil Company, which sold them at their western service stations. The chrome era continues; although in recent years, most postcards are being produced in 4″ by 6″ size rather than in the traditional 3.5″ by 5.5″ size. Figure 16 is of a chrome post-card of the Wayne County Courthouse in Waynesboro, Tennessee. Built in 1905, this concrete-block building, with stone trim, cupola, and clocks, burned in 1973.

With the exception of the postcards shown in figures 17 and 18, the postcards featured in the balance of this book are arranged under the

Fig. 15. Howard's Manor and Cottages, Millington.

Fig. 16. Wayne County Courthouse, Waynesboro.

Fig. 17. Coalmont.

Fig. 18. Gallatin.

following fourteen sections. Listed alphabetically, these sections are Agriculture, Bird's-Eye Views, Churches, Commerce and Industry, Homes, Hotels, Main Streets, Military, Parks and Recreation, People, Private Buildings, Public Buildings, Rivers and Streams, and Schools. Together, the sections display a cross section of the postcards in my collection. One group of postcards that didn't fit neatly into one of the fourteen sections contains generic postcards, which were published early in the twentieth century, often for towns so small that they did not have suitable buildings or landmarks as subjects for postcards. The post-cards of Coalmont and Gallatin, Tennessee, shown in figures 17 and 18, are examples.

Agriculture

Cotton and tobacco have traditionally been Tennessee's two leading crops. The state's cotton production has always has been centered in West Tennessee, although it is grown in Rutherford County as well as in the southern tier of Middle-Tennessee counties. In 1851, when Tennessee grew a far larger percentage of the cotton grown in the United States than it does now, Col. John Pope of Shelby County received a premium at the world's fair in London for having grown "the best cotton known to the world." Memphis is still one of the country's leading cotton markets.

Two types of tobacco are grown in Tennessee—dark-fired and burley. Clarksville and Springfield have traditionally been among the largest dark-fired tobacco markets in the country, while Greeneville continues to be one of the most important burley tobacco markets. The postcard of the Bell Witch Well at Adams, Tennessee (Fig. 1.1) shows a large field in the heart of Robertson County's tobacco belt.

During the first half of the twentieth century, other important Tennessee agricultural products were dairy cattle, corn, hay, hogs, vegetables, and wheat. The 1946 postcard view of Holston Valley (Fig. 1.15), where such products were grown, shows the Camp Hammond Bridge over the Holston River.

Humboldt and Portland were centers for the growing of strawberries. At times, Tennessee shipped more strawberries to market than any other state in the country. Mules were bred, raised, and sold, particularly in Giles, Maury, and Sumner Counties. Columbia still holds a Mule Day each spring (Fig. 1.5). The walking-horse industry is centered in Shelbyville (Fig. 1.26), where the extremely popular Tennessee Walking Horse Celebration is held annually. Sheep-raising is no longer important in Tennessee, but it once was. At the same world's fair in London where Col. Pope's Tennessee cotton received a premium, Mark Cockrill of Davidson County won a premium for having grown the best wool in the world.

Poultry production, however, continues to be an important source of income to Tennessee farmers. In January 1996 while attending parents' weekend at Vanderbilt Medical School, I spoke with my friend Robert W. Lowe Jr. of Cookeville, Tennessee. When I told Bob that I was working on a Tennessee postcard book, he mentioned having seen, years ago, a postcard of his grandfather, Jere Whitson, who was mayor of Cookeville before World War I. Bob said that Mr. Whitson and some Cookeville church leaders were posed with some chickens they intended to have served for dinner at the 1913 Tennessee Annual Conference of the Methodist Church. I told Bob that I not only had the postcard but was going to put it in the agriculture section of my book. When you look at figure 1.6, Mr. Whitson is the white-bearded gentleman on the left.

Fig. 1.1. *The Bell Witch Well, Adams.*

Fig. 1.2. *Ingleside Dairy, Athens.*

Fig. 1.3. *Fifth Annual Exhibition of the Clay County Fair Association, August 10–13, 1910, Celina.*

Fig. 1.4. Tobacco wagons, Clarksville.

Fig. 1.5. Mule Day, first Monday in April, Columbia.

Fig. 1.6. Preparing for the Tennessee Annual Conference of the Methodist Church, Cookeville.

15

Fig. 1.7. Highway U.S. 411 between Etowah and Benton.

Fig. 1.8. A stock day, Fayetteville.

Fig. 1.9. Picking strawberries, Gibson County.

Fig. 1.10. Elkmont Orchards, Great Smoky Mountains National Park.

Fig. 1.11. Farm products exhibited at Greene County Fair, 1910, Greeneville.

Fig. 1.12. Interior of a southern loose-leaf tobacco warehouse, Greeneville.

Fig. 1.13. Shipping tomatoes, Humboldt.

Fig. 1.14. Men's best friends at fair, October 12–16, 1909, Jackson.

Fig. 1.15. Aerial view of Holston Valley between Kingsport and Johnson City.

"THE OLD ELM" ON ROTHERWOOD FARM, NEAR KINGSPORT, TENN. OLD SILK MILL, IN REAR.

Fig. 1.16. "The Old Elm" on Rotherwood Farm, Kingsport (old silk mill in rear).

AIRPLANE VIEW, UNIVERSITY FARM, UNIVERSITY OF TENNESSEE   KNOXVILLE

Fig. 1.17. University Farm, University of Tennessee, Knoxville.

Fig. 1.18. Going a-milking, Liberty.

19

Fig. 1.19. Cotton-picking time, Memphis.

Fig. 1.20. Levee scene, cotton bales, Memphis.

Fig. 1.21. Loaded to the limit, Memphis.

Fig. 1.22. Millky Way Farm, Pulaski.

Fig. 1.23. Cotton scene, Ripley.

Fig. 1.24. Sheep camp, Roan Mountain.

LOVEDALE STOCK FARM, SAUNDERSVILLE, TENN.

Fig. 1.25. Lovedale Stock Farm, Saundersville.

SH-4—Tennessee Walking Horse National
Shelbyville, Tennessee

*Fig. 1.26. Tennessee Walking Horse National
Celebration Grounds, Shelbyville.*

Robertson County Tobacco Field, Springfield, Tenn.

*Fig. 1.27. Robertson County tobacco field,
Springfield.*

EWELL FARM, PUBLISHERS.   BIRD'S EYE VIEW OF EWELL FARM, SPRING HILL, TENN.

Fig. 1.28. Ewell Farm, Spring Hill.

They look like this in Sumner County, Tenn.

Fig. 1.29. Cows, Sumner County.

East Tennessee Fair at Sweetwater.   October 10, 11, 12, 13, 1911
SPECIAL ATTRACTIONS.   The Biggest Fair in East Tennessee in 1911

Fig. 1.30. East Tennessee Fair,
October 10–13, 1911, Sweetwater.

Fig. 1.31. Oxen and wagon, Tellico Plains.

Fig. 1.32. Fairgrounds, Union City.

Fig. 1.33. Peach Nursery, Winchester.

Bird's-Eye Views

There are not as many early bird's-eye views of Tennessee towns and cities as you might think. The reason is that airplanes were only in their infancy in the first two decades of the twentieth century and were seldom used to take aerial photographs of cities and towns. What appears to be an aerial view of Clarksville (Fig. 2.6) actually is a fanciful drawing of what someone, interested in Clarksville's image as a burgeoning manufacturing center, thought it might look like. The bird's-eye views of Bristol (Fig. 2.2), Coal Creek (Fig. 2.7), Columbia (Fig. 2.8), Johnson City, (Fig. 2.13), Knoxville (Fig. 2.15), Livingston (Fig. 2.17), Memphis (Fig. 2.19), Morristown (Fig. 2.22), Nashville (Fig. 2.23), Paris (Fig. 2.25), Rhea Springs (Fig. 2.26), and Somerville (Fig. 2.29) were all taken from nearby hills or convenient buildings—from the cupola on top of the State Capitol in Nashville's case. The scarcity of tall buildings and hills in West Tennessee explains why there were relatively few bird's-eye views of West Tennessee towns taken before 1940 other than those of Memphis (Fig. 2.21).

The postcard view of Bemis, Tennessee (Fig. 2.1), shows in the distance a four-story mill built by the Jackson Fibre Company in 1900. The owner of the company, Judson Moss Bemis, built the town around his mill as a means of securing a more stable work force. In addition to the white housing development, a portion of which is shown in the postcard, there was a separate housing development for blacks, a cotton gin,

a company store, schools, a public bathhouse, a YMCA, and a church. The postcard view of Sherwood (Fig. 2.28), another company town, is of particular interest to me since my wife and I have a summer cottage at nearby Monteagle, Tennessee. This former mining town, located in Franklin County on the railroad from Nashville to Chattanooga, is much smaller today than when this photograph was taken early in the twentieth century. The view of Coal Creek was taken a number of years before 1939, when the town's name legally changed to Lake City. That change seems appropriate because by then the coal mines were not nearly as productive as they had been earlier, and Norris Dam, built in 1936, had impounded a large and beautiful lake nearby. The true aerial views shown in this section are of Gatlinburg (Fig. 2.11), Memphis (Fig. 2.21), and Newport (Fig. 2.24). The Newport postcard is unusual because it was postmarked during the 1920s. The other three were published in the late 1930s.

The large structure in the foreground of the postcard view of Kingsport (Fig. 2.14) taken from Cement Hill was the Carolina, Clinchfield, & Ohio Railroad Depot, designed by New York architect Clinton McKenzie. Broad Street which runs north, is the avenue in the middle of the picture. Across the street from the railroad station, at the corner of Main and Broad, stood the two-story, colonnaded Bank of Kingsport. Fortunately, both it and the former railroad station have been preserved.

VIEW IN BEMIS, TENN. THE FINEST MILL VILLAGE IN SOUTHERN STATES

Fig. 2.1. *The finest mill village in the South, Bemis.*

Birds Eye View of Bristol, Tenn

Fig. 2.2. *Bristol.*

Looking into City from Williams and Myer Bridge, Carthage, Tennessee

Fig. 2.3. *Williams and Myer Bridge, Carthage.*

Fig. 2.4. View from Cameron Hill, Chattanooga.

Fig. 2.5. View from James Building, Chattanooga.

Fig. 2.6. Clarksville.

Fig. 2.7. Coal Creek.

Fig. 2.8. View from the Knob, Columbia.

Fig. 2.9. Elkmont.

Fig. 2.10. Looking northeast, Erin.

Fig. 2.11. Aerial view of Gatlinburg.

Fig. 2.12. Panoramic view, Huntsville.

29

BIRD'S EYE VIEW OF JOHNSON CITY, TENN.

Fig. 2.13. Johnson City.

Kingsport, Tenn., from Holston Heights.—1

Fig. 2.14. View from Holston Heights,
Kingsport.

KNOXVILLE, Tenn. Bird's-Eye View.

Fig. 2.15. Knoxville.

Fig. 2.16. View from the Empire Building, Knoxville.

Fig. 2.17. Livingston.

Fig. 2.18. Ben Lomond Mountain, McMinnville.

31

Fig. 2.19. Memphis.

Fig. 2.20. Approaching the Wharf, Memphis.

Fig. 2.21. Skyline view of Memphis.

Fig. 2.22. Morristown.

Fig. 2.23. Looking south from the Capitol, Nashville.

Fig. 2.24. Newport.

33

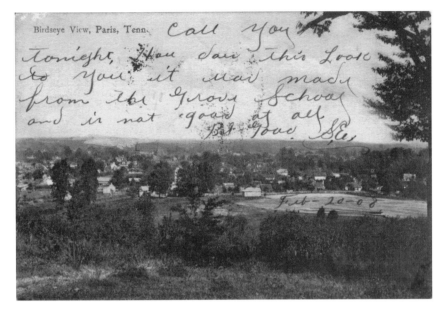

Fig. 2.25. Paris.

Fig. 2.26. Rhea Springs.

Fig. 2.27. Sevierville, named for the first governor of Tennessee.

Fig. 2.28. Sherwood.

Fig. 2.29. Somerville.

Fig. 2.30. Winchester.

Churches

In 1930, Tennessee had a population of 2,616,556, approximately half of whom were active church attendees. The Baptist, Methodist, Presbyterian, and Church of Christ congregations comprised, in that order, nearly 90 percent of the combined church membership. Late in the eighteenth century among the North Carolinians and Virginians in the Watauga, Holston, and Cumberland settlements were many Scots-Irish Presbyterians. The Baptists were also early arrivals on the Tennessee frontier. There is a story that the Baptists and Presbyterians in the Cumberland country arrived at an agreement under which the Presbyterians evangelized in the towns and the Baptists in the country. The fact that the first Baptist church in Nashville was not built until 1820 gives some credence to the story. In Dandridge, forty-five miles from Knoxville, the Presbyterian and Baptist Churches are actually older than the town, which was established in 1793. Hopewell Presbyterian Church (Fig. 3.13) was organized in 1785, while Dandridge Baptist Church was organized in 1786.

Although they started a little behind the Presbyterians and Baptists, the Methodists were very successful in recruiting members on the frontier. The Methodist circuit rider, with his Bible and hymnbook, was ideally suited for the task. Members of all three denominations took part in the Great Revival, which began in Southern Kentucky in the summer of 1800 and spread quickly to Middle Tennessee and then across the state. The revival seriously curtailed the growth of Presbyterians whose preachers called for their members to adhere to the discipline and doctrine of that faith rather than to adopt a new kind of emotional religion based on personal experience. By the time of the emergence of the Christian Church, the Presbyterians had fallen to the third-largest religious force in Tennessee. They were further weakened when the Cumberland Presbyterian Church was founded in 1810. Conversely, the Methodists shrewdly adapted their program to the frontier. From 1796 to 1800, the Methodists in Tennessee grew from 600 to 10,000.

Barton Warren Stone laid the foundation for the Christian Church in Tennessee. He preached and established churches in Davidson, Sumner, and Williamson Counties, patterning his activities somewhat along the lines of the Methodist circuit rider. Most of Stone's new members had been Presbyterians. In 1832, his group merged with a Restoration group led by Alexander Campbell, another former Presbyterian. The resulting group came to be variously known as the Christian Church, the Disciples of Christ, and the Churches of Christ. The Leipers Fork Church of Christ (Fig. 3.19) was built in 1877 on the site of the Union Meeting House, constructed in 1821. Under the influence of the Restoration movement and the preaching of Andrew Craig and Joel Anderson, Leipers Fork became the first Church of Christ south of Nashville. In 1862, David Lipscomb led a convention of Christians, who met at the church, to adopt positions as noncombatants in the Civil War. As you might imagine, their petition to military Gov. Andrew Johnson was not accepted.

In 1827, a Virginian, the Reverend James Hervey Otey, established St. Paul's Church in Franklin, the first

Episcopal congregation in Tennessee. The Episcopal Church's relatively late start in Tennessee can be largely attributed to the enmity that Scots-Irish, such as Andrew Jackson, held for the established Church of England. The Episcopal Church, which frowned on the emotionalism of the reform movement, gained most of its new members in towns and among well-to-do landowners.

The Catholic Church has also historically been a city church in Tennessee. Catholic priests made trips into Tennessee as early as 1810. That spring, the *Knoxville Gazette* announced that Rev. Stephen Theodore

Baden, a Roman Catholic priest from Kentucky, would preach at the Knox County Courthouse. The first organized Catholic service in Tennessee may have been held in Nashville in 1821.

The first Jewish congregation in Tennessee was organized in Memphis in 1852. The next year another was formed in Nashville. However, before the Civil War, there were fewer than 500 persons of Jewish faith in the state. Following the war, the religious spectrum in Tennessee broadened considerably. By 1926, 56 denominations and faiths, with 8,556 churches and 1,018,033 members, had been established in Tennessee.

Fig. 3.1. Central Presbyterian Church, Bristol.

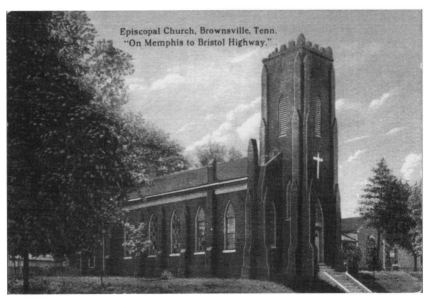

Fig. 3.2. Episcopal Church, Brownsville.

Fig. 3.3. Mizpah Temple, Chattanooga.

Fig. 3.4. Interior of Church of Sts. Peter and
Paul, Chattanooga.

Fig. 3.5. Bible Place, Cleveland.

Fig. 3.6. *Methodist Episcopal Church, Clarksville.*

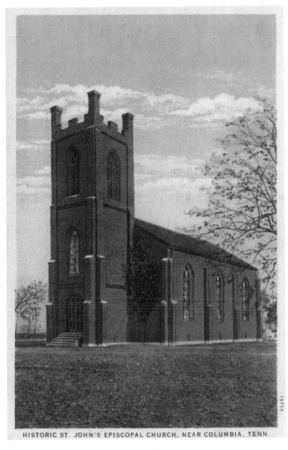

Fig. 3.7. *St. John's Episcopal Church between Columbia and Mt. Pleasant.*

Fig. 3.8. *Union Baptist Church, Dyersburg.*

Fig. 3.9. First Church of Christ, Columbia.

Fig. 3.10. Zion Presbyterian Church near Columbia.

Fig. 3.11. First Baptist Church, Covington.

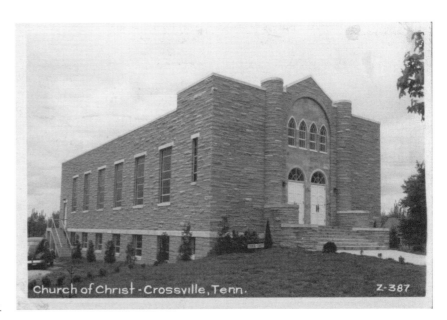

Fig. 3.12. *Church of Christ, Crossville.*

Fig. 3.13. *Hopewell Presbyterian Church, Dandridge.*

Fig. 3.14. *First Baptist Church, Erwin.*

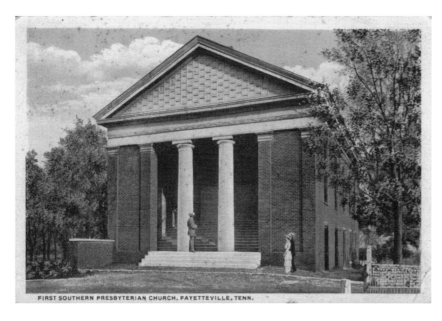

FIRST SOUTHERN PRESBYTERIAN CHURCH, FAYETTEVILLE, TENN.

Fig. 3.15. *First Southern Presbyterian Church, Fayetteville.*

PUBLISHED BY BRASFIELD'S DRUG STORE, PHOTO BY MRS. POWELL   MISSIONARY BAPTIST CHURCH, GREENFIELD, TENN.

Fig. 3.16. *Missionary Baptist Church, Greenfield.*

1923   FIRST BAPTIST CHURCH, JACKSON, TENN.

Fig. 3.17. *First Baptist Church, Jackson.*

Fig. 3.18. Methodist Church, Franklin.

B105385   Methodist Church, Franklin, Tenn.

Church of Christ, Leipers Fork, Tenn.

Fig. 3.19. Church of Christ, Leipers Fork.

First Methodist Church, Memphis, Tennessee
"Memphis Methodism's Mother Church"

Fig. 3.20. First Methodist Church, Memphis.

Fig. 3.21. Baptist Church, Jamestown.

Fig. 3.22. Munsey Memorial Methodist Episcopal Church, South, Johnson City.

Fig. 3.23. Civic Center and Church Circle, Kingsport.

44

CHURCH STREET M. E. CHURCH SOUTH. KNOXVILLE. TENN.

Fig. 3.24. Church Street Methodist Episcopal Church, South, Knoxville.

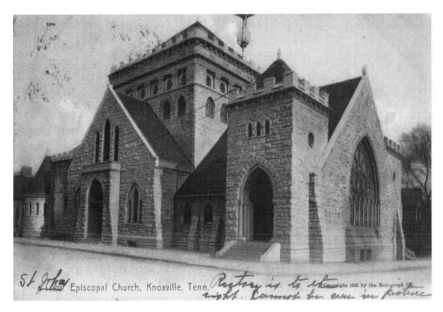

Episcopal Church, Knoxville, Tenn.

Fig. 3.25. Episcopal Church, Knoxville.

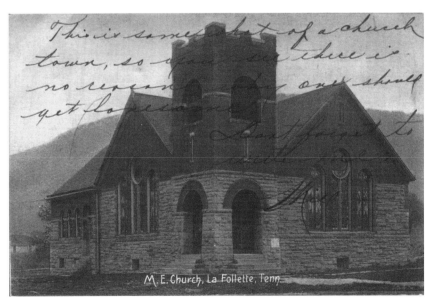

M. E. Church, La Follette, Tenn.

Fig. 3.26. Methodist Episcopal Church, LaFollette.

Fig. 3.27. *Cumberland Presbyterian Church, Lawrenceburg.*

Fig. 3.28. *Baptist Church, Martin.*

Fig. 3.29. *Interior of Central Baptist Church, Memphis.*

Fig. 3.30. *St. Mary's Cathedral, Memphis.*

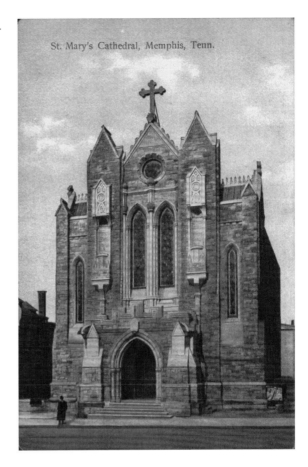

Fig. 3.31. *Second Presbyterian Church, Memphis.*

Fig. 3.32. *Five Christian churches and
Vine Street Temple, Nashville.*

"Rev. Spencer Tunnell First Baptist Church, Morristown, Tenn., Administering O...nance of Baptism at Shields Ferry, Holston River, May 11, 1913. Ninety-Se...Immersions in 55 Minutes."

Fig. 3.33. Rev. Spencer Tunnell, First Baptist Church, baptizes at Shields Ferry, Holston River, May 11, 1913, Morristown.

Fig. 3.34. Central Church of Christ, Murfreesboro.

Fig. 3.35. Seventh Day Adventists' Memorial Church, Nashville.

Fig. 3.36. First Lutheran Church, Nashville

First Lutheran Church, Nashville, Tennessee

St. Mary's Cathedral, Nashville, Tenn.

Fig. 3.37. St. Mary's Cathedral, Nashville.

Fig. 3.38. Christ Church, Rugby.

July 18 - 1907

PRSEBYTERIAN CHURCH OLIVER SPGS. TENN.

Fig. 3.39. Presbyterian Church, Oliver Springs.

Church of Christ, Paris, Tenn.

Fig. 3.40. Church of Christ, Paris.

FIRST METHODIST CHURCH, RIPLEY, TENN.

Fig. 3.41. First Methodist Church, Ripley.

Fig. 3.42. All Saints' Chapel, University of the South, Sewanee.

Fig. 3.43. First Christian Church, Union City.

Fig. 3.44. Methodist Church, Waverly.

51

Fig. 3.45. Cumberland Presbyterian Church, Union City.

Fig. 3.46. Cumberland Presbyterian Church, Winchester.

Fig. 3.47. Christian Church, Woodbury.

Commerce and Industry

At the beginning of the twentieth century, the manufacture of flour-mill and grist-mill products was Tennessee's most important industry. Mills, such as ones at Chuckey (Fig. 4.11) and Obion (Fig. 4.47), were found all over the state.

The manufacture of lumber and timber products was second in importance among Tennessee's industries in 1900. The postcard views of lumber mills and yards at Braemar (Fig. 4.3) and Memphis (Fig. 4.37) indicate how extensive these operations were. Similarly, Granges' Tobacco Warehouse in Clarksville (Fig. 4.12) testified to the importance of tobacco to that county's prosperity.

In 1900, ten Tennessee-based companies were manufacturing iron and steel. The state's principal iron-producing districts corresponded with the location of iron deposits. Postcards of LaFollette and Rockwood foundries (Figs. 4.30 and 4.53) speak to the industry's importance. Chattanooga was the center of Tennessee's coal and iron industry. The Tennessee Consolidated Coal Company in nearby Tracy City (Fig. 4.59) was one of the larger coal companies. Phosphate of commercial value was first discovered in Tennessee in 1893. Soon, companies built phosphate plants in Centerville (Fig. 4.7) and Mount Pleasant. Zinc mining at Jefferson City (Fig. 4.23), copper mining at Ducktown and Copper Hill, and marble quarries near Knoxville (Fig. 4.26) contributed handsomely to the state's economy. Foundries were vital to the well-being of Dayton, Chattanooga (Fig. 4.8), Cleveland (Fig. 4.13), and South Pittsburg (Fig. 4.57).

In the 1890s, Tennessee's textile industry was the smallest of the southern states and concentrated almost entirely in East and Middle Tennessee. Brookside Cotton Mill in Knoxville (Fig. 4.27) commenced operation in 1885. By 1910, its 60,000 spindles and 1,300 looms produced 6,500,000 pounds and 13 million yards of cotton goods, corduroy, velvet, and duck annually. Nashville's Warioto Cotton Mills (Fig. 4.45) evolved into the Werthan Bag Company, which was featured in the movie *Driving Miss Daisy*. Judson Moss Bemis's 21,000-spindle cotton mill (Fig. 4.2), three miles south of Jackson, took advantage of rural West Tennessee's largely untapped labor supply, proximity to the cotton belt, and ready access to the Illinois Central railroad tracks.

In 1900, Robertson County was as famous for its whiskey as for its tobacco. A much more famous producer of whiskey is in Moore County, where Jack Daniel first set up operations during the Civil War. By 1896, his was the largest sour-mash distillery in Tennessee. In 1904, Daniel took two cases of his old No. 7 whiskey to the world's fair in St. Louis where it was judged the finest in the world. An aerial view of the distillery, probably made during the 1930s, is shown in figure 4.33. In 1897, Nashville's William Gerst Brewing Company (Fig. 4.43) won the gold medal for its beer at the Tennessee Centennial Exposition. At that time, local brewers, such as Gerst, dominated Tennessee's beer market. Later, national brewers would put most of these companies out of business. Only in recent years have local brewing companies staged a comeback.

In West Tennessee, cottonseed oil and cake manufacturing concerns pumped dollars into such towns as Brownsville (Fig. 4.5), Ripley, and Trenton. The industry centered in Memphis, which in 1900 was the largest cottonseed oil market in the world (Fig. 4.36). By 1907, Jackson, the hub of West Tennessee, had its own automobile manufacturing company. William Collier's Southern Engine & Boiler Works (Fig. 4.22) produced about 400 cars in two styles between 1907 and 1910.

Across the state, railroad shops, engaged in the manufacture of railroad cars and in general shop work, were important contributors to Tennessee's economy. The Lenoir Car Works (Fig. 4.31) and the L & N Railroad Shop in Paris (Fig. 4.49) were good examples.

World War I saw an enormous powder plant established at Old Hickory near Nashville (Fig. 4.48). Almost immediately, postcards proclaimed Nashville as the "powder city of the world." In 1923, Dupont bought the plant to manufacture rayon. Another large rayon plant was in Elizabethton. In 1919, Alcoa, an acronym for Aluminum Company of America, was incorporated as a company town built around the North Maryville aluminum plant (Fig. 4.1).

Kingsport was the first thoroughly diversified, professionally planned, and privately financed city in twentieth-century America. Eastman Kodak Company officials announced their decision to build a plant there in 1920. By the depression, major expansions had propelled Tennessee Eastman (Fig. 4.24) into one of the state's largest industries. Among the products Tennessee Eastman manufactured were cellulose acetate, acetate yarn, and a plastic material called Tenite. The Kingsport Press (Fig. 4.25), which began construction in 1922, became another mainstay of the Kingsport economy.

Printing and publishing concerns in Nashville go back to the establishment of the Methodist Publishing House there in 1854. For many years, this establishment was located at 810 Broadway (Fig. 4.44).

In 1942, the U.S. government set aside a large area in Anderson and Roane Counties in what became the best-kept secret in the country. At one time, Oak Ridge's population rose to 83,000, yet almost no one knew that the atomic bomb was being produced there. As a child, my wife traveled with her mother to Oak Ridge from Nashville on the Tennessee Central Railroad to see her father, who was stationed there. Irene recalls waiting for what seemed like hours at a gate (Fig. 4.46) for her father to come and clear their entrance.

Postcard views of banks are included both in this and in the Private Buildings section of this book. The Chattanooga Savings Bank (Fig. 4.10) was organized in April 1889. The bank moved in 1908 into the new James Building (Fig. 11.6), where it had the largest and most convenient banking quarters of any bank in the city. In 1915, this institution was the largest savings bank in Tennessee with deposits of approximately three million dollars. All of the banks shown in this section were subsequently acquired by other banks. Knoxville's City National Bank (Fig. 4.29) was founded in 1888. In 1913, it controlled 24.5 percent of the city's national bank resources, ranking it second to the East Tennessee Bank in Knoxville. By 1921, City National Bank's share of resources grew to 28.7 percent, making it Knoxville's largest. City National was taken over by the East Tennessee National Bank in 1930.

Fig. 4.1. Reduction Plant, Aluminum Company of America, Alcoa.

View Showing North and East Sides of Mill, Bemis, Tenn.

Fig. 4.2. North and east sides of mill, Bemis.

Plant of the Pittsburg Lumber Co. at Braemar, Tenn.

Fig. 4.3. Plant of the Pittsburg Lumber Company, Braemar.

THE PURE FOOD COMPANY.

GOOD THINGS TO EAT.   BRISTOL. TENN.

Fig. 4.4. The Pure Food Company, Bristol.

Fig. 4.5. Brownsville Cotton Oil and Ice Company, Brownsville.

Fig. 4.6. Sampson Sanitarium and Mineral Wells, Carthage.

Fig. 4.7. Standard G. R. Phosphate Company Plant, Centerville.

Fig. 4.8. Lookout Mountain from Cameron Hill,
now Boynton Park, Chattanooga.

Fig. 4.9. Johnny Green, in his Cardui
Flyer, flying near Lookout Mountain and
over the laboratories of the Chattanooga
Medicine Company, Chattanooga.

Fig. 4.10. Interior of banking room, the
Chattanooga Savings Bank, Chattanooga.

Fig. 4.11. The Mill, Chuckey.

Fig. 4.12. Granges' Tobacco Warehouse,
Clarksville.

Fig. 4.13. Dixie Foundry Company, Cleveland.

Fig. 4.14. Dixie Portland Cement Plant, Copenhagen.

Fig. 4.15. American Glanzstoff Corporation, Elizabethton.

Fig. 4.16. P. A. Kinser's Drug Store, Etowah.

THE SUMNER COUNTY BANK & TRUST CO. BUILDING, GALLATIN, TENNESSEE.

Fig. 4.17. The Sumner County Bank & Trust Company Building, Gallatin.

BALES CABINS ON BASKINS CREEK - GATLINBURG, TENN.

Fig. 4.18. Bales Cabins on Baskins Creek, Gatlinburg.

Fig. 4.19. Oliver Hale & Company, Gibson.

CAPITOL SERVICE STATION, GREENEVILLE, TENN.

Fig. 4.20. Capitol Service Station, Greeneville.

THOMPSON SHOE FACTORY, HUMBOLDT, TENN.

Fig. 4.21. Thompson Shoe Factory, Humboldt.

Fig. 4.22. Southern Engine & Boiler Works,
Jackson.

The Mill Scene, Zinc Mines in background, Jefferson City, Tenn.

Fig. 4.23. Mill scene, zinc mines in background, Jefferson City.

K-33.   AIRPLANE VIEW OF TENNESSEE EASTMAN COMPANY, KINGSPORT, TENN.

Fig. 4.24. View of Tennessee Eastman Company, Kingsport.

KINGSPORT PRESS, KINGSPORT, TENN.—7

Fig. 4.25. Kingsport Press, Kingsport.

Fig. 4.26. Marble quarry, Knoxville.

Fig. 4.27. Brookside Cotton Mill, Knoxville.

Fig. 4.28. Rexall Store, Knoxville.

City National Bank, Interior Knoxville, Tenn.   City National Bank, Exterior Knoxville, Tenn.

Fig. 4.29. Interior and exterior views of City National Bank, Knoxville.

This is a beautiful country, and the climate healthful, and beneficial Mill.

Blast Furnace, La Follette, Tenn.

Fig. 4.30. Blast Furnace, LaFollette.

49122   LENOIR CAR WORKS, LENOIR CITY, TENN.

Fig. 4.31. Lenoir Car Works, Lenoir City.

Fig. 4.32. Lewisburg Light Plant, Lewisburg.

Fig. 4.33. Jack Daniel Distillery, Lynchburg.

Fig. 4.34. Meeks Mercantile Company,
September 1907, Meeks.

Fig. 4.35. *Cotton Exchange and Cotton Arch on Second Street, Memphis.*

Fig. 4.36. *Cottonseed oil mill, Memphis.*

Fig. 4.37. *One of the many lumber mills and yards, Memphis.*

THIS immense fireproof steel and concrete building, with brick and stone trimmings, was officially reported by the Tennessee Factory Inspector at 100 per cent—this means that it is perfect as a model in hygiene and efficiency. In it all Rawleigh Products sold in the South are made. It is noted for its architectural excellence. Its five light and airy floors are equipped better than any similar plant in the South. It has the largest number of employes of any similar industry in Memphis. It carries the largest stocks, produces the greatest number and variety of Products sold in the South.

Fig. 4.38. The W. T. Rawleigh Company, Memphis.

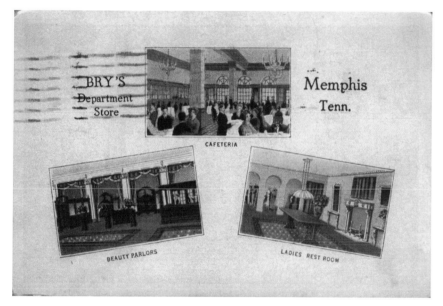

Fig. 4.39. Bry's Department Store, Memphis.

Fig. 4.40. Milan Shirt Factory, Milan.

Fig. 4.41. Carnation Milk Products
Condensery, Murfreesboro.

Fig. 4.42. Maxwell House Shoe Company, 517
Church Street, Nashville.

Fig. 4.43. William Gerst Brewing Company,
Nashville.

Fig. 4.44. Publishing House, M. E. Church,
South, 810 Broadway, Nashville.

Fig. 4.45. Warioto Cotton Mills, Nashville.

Fig. 4.46. Clinton Engineering Works,
Oak Ridge.

Fig. 4.47. Obion Mill and Elevator Company, Obion.

Fig. 4.48. Dupont Plant, Old Hickory.

Fig. 4.49. L & N Railway Shop, Paris.

Fig. 4.50. J. R. Spicer, funeral director, Paris.

Fig. 4.51. Bank of Perryville, Perryville.

Fig. 4.52. G. D. McCrary, Philadelphia.

Fig. 4.53. Iron Furnaces, Rockwood.

Fig. 4.54. Dixie Cafe, Selmer.

Fig. 4.55. Sylvan Cotton Mills, Shelbyville.

GRILL 64 & FOUNTAIN — IN CITY On U.S. 64 — Somerville, Tenn.

Fig. 4.56. Grill 64 & Fountain, Somerville.

THE H. WETTER MANUFACTURING COMPANY, SOUTH PITTSBURG, TENN.

Fig. 4.57. The H. Wetter Manufacturing Company, South Pittsburg.

Shipping a car load of Blankets from Springfield Woolen Mills.

Fig. 4.58. Shipping blankets from Springfield Woolen Mills, Springfield.

73

Fig. 4.59. Palmer Processing Plant, Tracy City.

Fig. 4.60. M. R. Campbell Hub and Spoke Factory, Tullahoma.

Fig. 4.61. The Jeff J. Blanks Company Department Store, Trezevant.

74

Homes

Postcard images in this section include the homes of many prominent Tennesseans, including those of Tennessee's three U.S. presidents—Andrew Jackson (Fig. 5.28), James K. Polk (Fig. 5.8), and Andrew Johnson (Fig. 5.11). In the postcard image of Jackson's Hermitage, notice that President Theodore Roosevelt is standing on the balcony in the center of the picture. Among those present at the presidential reception held October 22, 1907, was Mrs. Rachel Jackson Lawrence, the daughter of Gen. Andrew Jackson's adopted son, Andrew Jr.

Also included are postcard views of Blount Mansion, home of William Blount (Fig. 5.16), southwest territorial governor, and the homes of seven Tennessee governors. The gubernatorial homes shown are those of William G. Brownlow (Fig. 5.17), William Prentice Cooper (Fig. 5.36), Isham G. Harris (Fig. 5.40) Albert S. Marks (Fig. 5.41), James D. Porter (5.32), John Sevier (Fig. 5.18), and Robert Love Taylor (Fig. 5.15). Governor Marks's home in Winchester, Hundred Oaks, was converted by his son Arthur Handly Marks into an old-world castle, complete with a seventy-five foot tower.

Also shown are the homes of Knoxville founder James White (Fig. 5.19); U.S. Senator Estes Kefauver (Fig. 5.21); World War I hero Sgt. Alvin York (Fig. 5.31); Secretary of State Cordell Hull (Fig. 5.5), and Cherokee Indian Chief John Walker (Fig. 5.7). The homes of two prominent American women are also shown: Metropolitan Opera star Grace Moore's childhood home (Fig. 5.14) in Jellico and the childhood home of Jean Faircloth McArthur, wife of Gen. Douglas McArthur, in Murfreesboro (5.26).

The postcard of the McClure House in Altamont, Tennessee, (Fig. 5.1) is the only one I have ever seen of the Grundy county seat. There are, however, numerous postcards of Beersheba Springs, the summer resort a few miles from Altamont. I have chosen a postcard showing the Howell Cottage (Fig. 5.2), one of twenty built by Beersheba Springs's founder John Armfield. In 1873, the cottage was bought by Mrs. Morton B. Howell and her sister Lucy Wilkins and has been owned by Howell descendants ever since. In the 1911 photograph, Betty Weaver and Maude Howell are sitting on the steps.

Carnton Plantation (Fig. 5.9), the home of the McGavock family, gained its status as a southern shrine on the morning following the fateful Battle of Franklin when the bodies of Confederate Generals—Cleburne, Adams, Granbury, and Strahl—lay dead on the back porch. Belle Meade (Fig. 5.27), the queen of Tennessee plantations, was the scene of fighting on the first day of the Battle of Nashville. Civil War history set its mark on Cherry Mansion (Fig. 5.35) in Savannah, Tennessee, when Gen. U. S. Grant made his headquarters there in April 1862. He was having breakfast at Cherry Mansion when the sound of heavy firing warned him that the Battle of Shiloh was underway. The Henry Spofford House (Fig. 5.33) in Pulaski was where the Ku Klux Klan was organized in December 1865 and where all of its earliest meetings were held. The home was then owned by Spofford's father-in-law, Thomas Martin, a prominent Pulaski citizen and founder of Martin College. Martin never knew that his home was the birthplace of the Ku Klux Klan, as he and his family were out of town when it was founded.

Representing Chattanooga in this section is a view of Oak Street (Fig. 5.6) and Stonedge (Fig. 5.20), the residence of Mr. and Mrs. J. B. Pound of Lookout Mountain. Langley Hall (Fig. 5.10) near Gallatin was the largest wood frame residence ever erected in Sumner County. It was built in 1903 by Kate Trousdale. The Barnette Home in Harriman (Fig. 5.12) is interesting because it was the home of an African-American family. Such postcards are rare. State Senator Daniel Cooper Swab's home (Fig. 5.13) was in Hartranft, Tennessee. He was a member of Tennessee's General Assembly from 1909 to 1911 and president of the Middlesboro Coal Company. Hartranft is a hamlet in nearby Claiborne County, Tennessee.

Memphis is represented by grocery entrepreneur Clarence Saunders's thirty-two-room mansion constructed of pink marble (Fig. 5.23). In 1929, the City of Memphis converted the Chickasaw Gardens home into a municipal museum called the Pink Palace. Wren's Nest, on the bluff at Monteagle, (Fig. 5.24), is owned by Mrs. Joseph Handly. The house was built in 1906. Each June, the internationally known financier Sir John Templeton, a cousin of Mrs. Handly's husband, holds a meeting of the Templeton Foundation there.

My final story of this section concerns Manor Hall (Fig. 5.25), built in 1849 in Mount Pleasant by Martin Luther Stockard. Rev. and Mrs. John Stevenson Frierson later owned the house. The little boy sitting on his pony in front of the house was John Stevenson Frierson III, their grandson. One day, when John and his friend Alden H. Smith were on their ponies in front of the house, John fell off. The pony was so docile and well-trained that he lifted his hoof until the little boy could be picked up.

The Mc Clure House in Altamont, the County seat on the Cumberland Plateau.

Fig. 5.1. The McClure House, Altamont.

Fig. 5.2. Howell Cottage, Beersheba Springs.

Fig. 5.3. The Bills Home, The Pillars, Bolivar.

Fig. 5.4. Residence, Camden.

Fig. 5.5. Cordell Hull Home, Carthage.

77

Fig. 5.6. Oak Street, looking west, Chattanooga.

Fig. 5.7. Chief John Walker House, Cleveland.

Fig. 5.8. Ancestral home of President James Knox Polk, Columbia.

Fig. 5.9. Carnton Plantation, Franklin.

LANGLEY HALL, GALLATIN, TENN.

Fig. 5.10. Langley Hall, Gallatin.

Fig. 5.11. Later residence of President Andrew
Johnson, Greeneville.

5136 The Barnette Home, Harriman, Tenn.

Fig. 5.12. Barnette Home, Harriman.

Bungalow of Senator Daniel Cooper Swab, Hartranft, Tenn.

Fig. 5.13. Bungalow of Senator Daniel Cooper Swab, Hartranft.

HOME OF GRACE MOORE

Fig. 5.14. Home of Grace Moore, Jellico.

80

Birthplace of Robt. L. Taylor, near Johnson City, Tenn.—9

Fig. 5.15. Birthplace of Robert L. Taylor near Johnson City.

DRAWING ROOM IN BLOUNT MANSION, KNOXVILLE, TENN. PORTRAITS OF TERRITORIAL GOV. WM. BLOUNT (LEFT) AND HIS HALF BROTHER WILLIE BLOUNT WHO WAS GOVERNOR OF THE STATE OF TENNESSEE 3 CONSECUTIVE TERMS. ORIGINAL MANTELPIECE

Fig. 5.16. Drawing room in Blount Mansion, Knoxville.

14203—
Residence
of Gov. N. G.
Brownlow,
Cumberland
Ave.
East Knoxville,
Tenn.

Fig. 5.17. Residence of Gov. W. G. Brownlow, Knoxville.

Fig. 5.18. Home of John Sevier near Knoxville.

Fig. 5.19. First house in Knoxville built by Gen. James White, 1786, Knoxville.

Fig. 5.20. Stonedge, residence of Mr. and Mrs. J. B. Pound, Lookout Mountain.

Fig. 5.21. Kefauver Home and Dairy Farm,
Madisonville.

Fig. 5.22. Gardner Home, Martin.

Fig. 5.23. Pink Palace in Chickasaw Gardens,
Memphis.

Fig. 5.24. Wren's Nest, Monteagle.

*Fig. 5.25. Manor Hall, residence of
J. S. Frierson, Mount Pleasant.*

*Fig. 5.26. Childhood home of Mrs. Douglas
McArthur, Murfreesboro.*

Fig. 5.27. Belle Meade Plantation, Nashville.

Fig. 5.28. The Hermitage, home of President Andrew Jackson, Nashville.

Fig. 5.29. Polk Place, home of President James K. Polk, Nashville.

Fig. 5.30. Residence of A. Wilson, Obion.

Fig. 5.31. Home of Sgt. Alvin C. York, Pall Mall.

Fig. 5.32. Antebellum residence of Gov. James D. Porter, Paris.

Spofford House, Pulaski, Tenn.
Where Ku Klux Klan was organized.

Fig. 5.33. Henry Spofford House, Pulaski.

Newbury House - Rugby, Tenn.

Fig. 5.34. Newbury House, Rugby.

Cherry Residence (Grant's Headquarters during Shiloh Battle).

Fig. 5.35. Cherry Mansion, Savannah.

RESIDENCE, MR. WM. P. COOPER, SHELBYVILLE, TENN.

Fig. 5.36. Residence of William P. Cooper, Shelbyville.

SAM DAVIS HOME Smurna, Tenn.
Compliments of Sam Davis Home chapter U.D.C.

Fig. 5.37. Sam Davis Home, Smyrna.

"The Famous Rock House"
Stopping Place of Presidents
during Stage Coach Days
In the Cumberland Mountains
Near Sparta, Tennessee

Fig. 5.38. Rock House, Sparta.

Fig. 5.39. High Street, Trenton.

HIGH STREET, TRENTON, TENN.

BIRTH PLACE OF ISHAM G. HARRIS, THREE MILES FROM TULLAHOMA, TENN.

Fig. 5.40. Birthplace of Isham G. Harris, Tullahoma.

Fig. 5.41. Hundred Oaks, birthplace of Albert S. Marks, Winchester.

THE HUNDRED OAKS, A BEAUTIFUL HOME, WINCHESTER, TENN.

*H*otels

For many children growing up during the 1940s and 1950s within a 150-mile radius of Memphis, the Peabody Hotel, completed in 1925, personified the glamour and grandeur of the state's largest city. Its ornate lobby (Fig. 6.26) was said to be where the Mississippi Delta started. A predecessor hotel, the original Peabody (Fig. 6.23) faced Main Street at the corner of Monroe. It burned in the mid-1920s.

Just as the Peabody seemed to many West Tennesseans to anchor their end of the state, two East Tennessee hotels—the Read House in Chattanooga (Fig. 6.5) and the Andrew Johnson Hotel in Knoxville (Fig. 6.8)—were almost as well-known. In Nashville, members of the state legislature and Vanderbilt-Tennessee football fans often stayed at the elegant, beaux-arts Hermitage Hotel (Fig. 6.33). Three of these hotels—the Peabody, the Hermitage, and the Read House—remain popular today.

Early in the twentieth century, resort hotels at such watering spas as Beersheba Springs (Fig. 6.2), Bloomington Springs, Primm Springs, Red Boiling Springs (Fig. 6.36), and Tate Spring (Fig. 6.32) bragged about their scenery and good food. Most of them also boasted of their relatively high altitude, cool air, and fine mineral water. Tate Spring, located near Rutledge, was one of the country's finest health spas and resorts during this period. It attracted such familes as the Rockefellers, Fords, Firestones, and Studebakers. The depression caused its closure in 1936, and twenty-seven years later the hotel burned.

Many hotels in small towns, such as the Sedberry in McMinnville (Fig. 6.20) and the Hale Springs Inn in Rogersville, were also well-known for their southern

cooking. During the 1940s, affluent Nashville families thought nothing of driving to McMinnville for Sunday dinner at the Sedberry.

Because railroads did not normally have dining cars in the early years of the twentieth century, hotels in such railroad towns as Cowan, Etowah, Hickman (Fig. 6.15), and Milan (Fig. 6.27) catered to passengers traveling by rail. Other hotels in industrial towns, such as Kingston or South Pittsburg, were favored by traveling salesmen. Called drummers ninety years ago, these men normally came by train, often from one of the large wholesale houses in Memphis or Nashville.

With the advent of better roads, the Monteagle Hotel (Fig. 6.28) boasted that its location on U.S. 41 was at the highest point and equidistant between Chicago and Miami. Chattanooga's Patten Hotel (Fig. 6.6) took advantage of its strategic location at the intersection of three key U.S. highways. The Rhea-Mims Hotel in Newport heralded its location on the Dixie Highway.

For many decades, a few local business people and a handful of elderly widows and spinsters could be found as permanent residents of many of the smaller hotels across the state. A great aunt of mine spent her declining years in relative comfort at the Dixie Hotel in Shelbyville (Fig.6.39).

Often our hotels were named for famous Tennesseans. Examples were the John Sevier in Johnson City (Fig. 6.17), the Cordell Hull in Carthage, the James K. Polk in Murfreesboro (Fig. 6.29), and the Davy Crockett in Union City (Fig. 6.41). Many boys from Madison County thought Jackson's New Southern Hotel (Fig. 6.16) was just about the finest one they could imagine and certainly one of the tallest.

Other Tennesseans recall going to dances at the General Shelby in Bristol, the Chisca in Memphis (Fig. 6.22), or the Maxwell House in Nashville (Fig. 6.34). Early in the twentieth century, Columbia socialites enjoyed dances at the Bethell House (Fig. 6.11), a smaller version of Nashville's famous Maxwell House.

As roads became better, Tennessee's hotels felt increasing competition from tourist homes. With the advent of the modern motel chains, many hotels either closed or were converted into apartments. Some, such as the Lookout Inn and the John Sevier, suffered disastrous fires, while others have long since been torn down and replaced with parking lots. Of all the hotels shown in this section, only a few remain.

5803 Hotel Magill, Athens, Tenn.

Fig. 6.1. Hotel Magill, Athens.

Fig. 6.2. Beersheba Springs Hotel,
Beersheba Springs.

HOTEL BRISTOL, BRISTOL, TENN.

Fig. 6.3. Hotel Bristol, Bristol.

Dining Room.
Hotel Patten.
Chattanooga's
Million Dollar Hotel,
Chattanooga, Tenn.

Fig. 6.4. Dining room, Hotel Patten,
Chattanooga.

CHATTANOOGA, Tenn. Read House

Fig. 6.5. Read House, Chattanooga.

Fig. 6.6. Hotel Patten, Chattanooga.

Fig. 6.6. Hotel Patten, Chattanooga.

Fig. 6.7. Hotel Lindo, Covington.

Fig. 6.8. Hotel Andrew Johnson, Knoxville.

Fig. 6.9. Arlington Hotel, Clarksville.

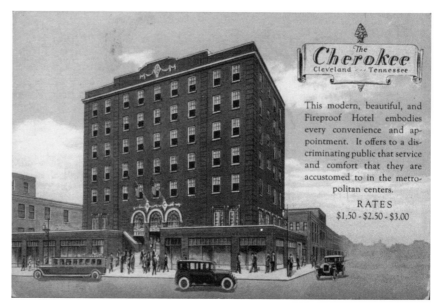

Fig. 6.10. Cherokee Hotel, Cleveland.

Fig. 6.11. Bethell House, Columbia.

Fig. 6.12. Hotel Atwood, Dyersburg.

Fig. 6.13. Grounds of the Gibson Wells Hotel, Gibson Wells.

Fig. 6.14. Hotel Harriman, 1923, Harriman.

Fig. 6.15. Huddleston House, Hickman.

Fig. 6.16. New Southern Hotel, Jackson.

Fig. 6.17. Hotel John Sevier, Johnson City.

96

Fig. 6.18. Kingsport Inn, Kingsport.

Fig. 6.19. Hotel Atkin, Knoxville.

Fig. 6.20. Sedberry Hotel, McMinnville.

Fig. 6.21. Stratford Hotel, Knoxville.

Fig. 6.22. Hotel Chisca, Memphis.

Fig. 6.23. Peabody Hotel, Memphis.

Fig. 6.24. First hotel in Memphis before the
Civil War, Memphis.

Fig. 6.25. Gayoso Hotel, Memphis.

Fig. 6.26. Lobby of the Peabody Hotel,
Memphis.

Southern Pacific Hotel, Milan, Tenn.

Fig. 6.27. Southern Pacific Hotel, Milan.

Monteagle Hotel, Monteagle, Tenn.

Fig. 6.28. Monteagle Hotel, Monteagle.

JAMES K. POLK
Eleventh President
of the United States

JAMES K. POLK HOTEL,
MURFREESBORO, TENN.

Fig. 6.29. James K. Polk Hotel, Murfreesboro.

Fig. 6.30. Hotel Cumberland, Monterey.

MONTEREY, TENN.   Hotel Cumberland

1993 Duncan Hotel, Nashville, Tenn.

Sister

Fig. 6.31. Duncan Hotel, Nashville.

Chestnut Spring and East Corner Tate Spring Hotel, Tate Spring, Tenn.

Fig. 6.32. Tate Spring Hotel, Tate Spring.

Fig. 6.33. The Loggia, Hermitage Hotel, Nashville.

Fig. 6.34. Maxwell House, Nashville.

Fig. 6.35. Colonial Hotel, New Market.

Fig. 6.36. Palace Hotel, Red Boiling Springs.

Fig. 6.37. Roan Mountain Inn,
Roan Mountain.

Fig. 6.38. New Central Hotel, Sevierville.

Fig. 6.39. Hotel Dixie, Shelbyville.

Fig. 6.40. Hotel Colonial, Springfield.

Fig. 6.41. Hotel Davy Crockett, Union City.

104

Main Streets

The six streets in Tennessee which appear most frequently in my postcard collection are State Street in Bristol, Market Street in Chattanooga, Franklin Street in Clarksville, Gay Street in Knoxville, Main Street in Memphis, and Church Street in Nashville. All are shown in this section. The postcard picture of Franklin Street (Fig. 7.5) seems to have been taken on a Saturday, the day on which farmers and their families traditionally came to county seats to buy clothes and supplies, gossip, and trade and sell their products. Other postcards show near-deserted streets. They remind me of the story told during the presidential election of 1828 between Andrew Jackson and John Quincy Adams. It seems a North Carolina legislator came into a small Tennessee town puzzled to find no one about. He went to a saloon and asked the bartender where everyone was. The proprietor said that the men had all left town, hunting for the two scoundrels who voted for Adams. Tennessee's popular vote in the election was approximately 44,000 votes for Jackson and about 2,200 for Adams. In many towns, Jackson received every vote.

Whenever I see a postcard of State Street (Fig. 7.2), I think about the summer day in 1927 when the father of country music, Jimmy Rodgers, recorded his first number, "Sleep, Baby, Sleep," for a Victor talent agent in Bristol. While Rodgers was recording in a second-floor room of a brick building on the Tennessee side of the street, his wife and daughter watched from the window of their hotel room across State Street in Virginia.

The postcard photograph of Johnson City's crowded Main Street (Fig. 7.35) was taken on the Fourth of July 1908. The postcard of Knoxville's Gay Street (Fig. 7.40) was taken during the election of 1904, when Republican presidential candidate Theodore Roosevelt defeated the Democratic standard-bearer, Judge Alton B. Parker of New York. A banner over Gay Street carries Teddy Roosevelt's likeness. The postcards of Nashville's Church Street (Figs. 7.41 and 7.42) were made in 1918 just after the powder plant opened at nearby Old Hickory.

The statue in the center of the postcard picture of Lebanon's Public Square (Fig. 7.43) is of Confederate Gen. Robert H. Hatton, an extremely popular former congressman who was killed at the Battle of Seven Pines in May 1862. Finally, notice the postcard of Memphis's Main Street (Fig. 7.53) made about 1912. The electric street cars, pedestrians, bicyclists, horse-drawn vehicles, and automobiles all seem to be vying for space. Memphis was riding high—cotton was king, E. H. Crump was mayor, W. C. Handy was singing the blues, and Memphians were confident and excited about their future. Memphis was quickly taking on the trappings of a modern twentieth-century city.

Fig. 7.1. Main Street, Bells.

Fig. 7.2. State Street, Bristol.

Fig. 7.3. Brownsville Cotton Market, Brownsville.

Fig. 7.4. Market Street, Chattanooga.

Fig. 7.5. Franklin Street, Clarksville.

Fig. 7.6. Northeast view from courthouse,
Cleveland.

Fig. 7.7. Depot Street, Cookeville.

Fig. 7.8. River Street, Copperhill.

Fig. 7.9. West side of Public Square, Covington.

Fig. 7.10. Crossville.

Fig. 7.11. Main Street, Dandridge.

Fig. 7.12. Dayton.

109

Fig. 7.13. Main Street, Decherd.

Fig. 7.14. Main Street, looking north, Dickson.

Fig. 7.15. Main Street, Ducktown.

Fig. 7.16. Mill Street, Dyersburg.

Fig. 7.17. Elk Avenue, Elizabethton.

Fig. 7.18. Main Street, looking north,
Estill Springs.

111

Fig. 7.19. Etowah.

Fig. 7.20. School Day, Fayetteville.

Fig. 7.21. Main Street, Franklin.

Fig. 7.22. Main Street, looking east, Gatlinburg.

Fig. 7.23. Dresden Street, looking north, Greenfield.

Fig. 7.24. Roane Street, looking north, Harriman.

113

MAIN STREET, HARTSVILLE, TENN.

Fig. 7.25. Main Street, Hartsville.

Street Scene - Henderson, Tenn.

F-I

Fig. 7.26. Henderson.

Main Street Looking East, Hohenwald, Tenn.

Fig. 7.27. Main Street, looking east, Hohenwald.

Fig. 7.28. Main Street, looking north, Greeneville.

Fig. 7.29. Main Street, looking west, Huntington.

Fig. 7.30. Wall Avenue, looking west, Knoxville.

MAIN STREET, LOOKING EAST, HUMBOLDT, TENN.

Fig. 7.31. *Main Street, looking east, Humboldt.*

St. Scene - Jacksboro, Tenn.   1-S-302

Fig. 7.32. *Jacksboro.*

MARKET ST. LOOKING SOUTH, JACKSON, TENN.

Fig. 7.33. *Market Street, looking south, Jackson.*

Fig. 7.34. Jasper.

Fig. 7.35. Main Street, Johnson City.

Fig. 7.36. Main Street, looking west, Jonesboro.

Fig. 7.37. Broad Street, Kingsport.

Fig. 7.38. Main Street, Lafayette.

Fig. 7.39. Opera house block, LaFollette.

118

Fig. 7.40. East side of Gay Street, Knoxville.

Fig. 7.41. Church Street, looking west, Nashville, 1918.

Fig. 7.42. Church Street, looking east, Nashville, 1918.

Fig. 7.43. Public Square, looking west,
Lebanon.

Fig. 7.44. A. Street, Lenoir City.

Fig. 7.45. West End Boulevard, Lewisburg.

120

Fig. 7.46. Court Square, Lexington.

Fig. 7.47. Loudon.

Fig. 7.48. McKenzie.

Fig. 7.49. Main Street, McMinnville.

Fig. 7.50. Madisonville.

Fig. 7.51. Lindell Street, Martin.

Fig. 7.52. Main Street, looking east, Maryville.

Fig. 7.53. Main Street, Memphis.

Fig. 7.54. Skyscrapers, Memphis.

MAIN STREET LOOKING SOUTH. MILAN, TENNESSEE.   H-610

Fig. 7.55. Main Street, looking south, Milan.

RAILROAD AVENUE.   MONTEAGLE, TENN.

Fig. 7.56. Railroad Avenue, Monteagle.

MAIN STREET, LOOKING WEST, BY NIGHT, MORRISTOWN, TENN.

Fig. 7.57. Main Street, looking west, Morristown.

Main Street, looking East   Mountain City, Tennessee   "Where Life Is Better"

Fig. 7.58. Main Street, looking east,
Mountain City.

Main Street, Looking South, Mt. Pleasant, Tenn.

Fig. 7.59. Main Street, looking south,
Mt. Pleasant.

Fig. 7.60. Murfreesboro.

A VIEW OF MAIN STREET, NEWPORT, TENN.

Fig. 7.61. Main Street, Newport.

MARKET STREET, PARIS, TENN.

Fig. 7.62. Market Street, Paris.

LOOKING NORTH ON FIRST STREET, PULASKI, TENNESSEE

Fig. 7.63. First Street, looking north, Pulaski.

Fig. 7.64. West side of Public Square,
looking north, Ripley.

Fig. 7.65. Rockwood Avenue, Rockwood.

Fig. 7.66. Main Street, Rogersville.

127

Fig. 7.67. Village Street, Sewanee.

Fig. 7.68. Sparta.

Fig. 7.69. Main Street, looking south, Spring Hill.

Fig. 7.70. Public Square, east side, Springfield.

Fig. 7.71. Public Square, Trenton.

Fig. 7.72. Lincoln Street, Tullahoma.

129

FIRST STREET, LOOKING NORTH, UNION CITY, TENN.

Fig. 7.73. First Street, looking north, Union City.

B1552F6   Church Street, Waverly, Tenn.   W. T. McCracken, Druggist.

Fig. 7.74. Church Street, Waverly.

Home Bank and Southwest Side Public Square, Winchester, Tenn. 5531

Fig. 7.75. Home Bank and southwest side Public Square, Winchester.

Military

From the first white settlement of Tennessee in 1769 until the end of the Indian Wars in 1795, life in the Volunteer State was dark and bloody. Early heroes in the Indian wars included Daniel Boone, John Sevier, and James Robertson. Soon after Robertson and John Donelson's settlement of Nashville in 1780, an epic Indian fight took place there. It would become celebrated in Tennessee history books as the Battle of the Bluffs. The tough settlers of what is now Middle Tennessee were too busy maintaining their tenuous toehold on the Cumberland to participate in the famous Battle of Kings Mountain, which took place in October 1780 in South Carolina. There, Overmountain Men from the Holston and Watauga settlements, aided by Col. William Campbell and his Virginians, defeated Maj. Patrick Ferguson in a victory that turned the tide of the Revolutionary War in the South.

Tennesseans were proud to fight under Gen. Andrew Jackson during the War of 1812. They were with him at New Orleans where his crushing victory over the overconfident English brought Jackson international fame and eventually propelled him into the presidency of the United States.

The next military heroes to emerge from the Tennessee mist were David Crockett and Sam Houston, one a Tennessee congressman and the other a Tennessee governor. Crockett, who went to Texas after losing a Tennessee congressional race, died a hero at the Alamo in 1836. Houston left Tennessee in 1829 to gain fame as defeater of Gen. Santa Anna. Houston was general of the Texas army, president of the Republic of Texas, U.S. senator from Texas, and governor of Texas.

During the Mexican War of 1846–1848, Tennessee was called on to provide 2,800 men. Thirty thousand volunteered. Our state's overwhelming response reconfirmed its nickname, "Volunteer State," earned during the War of 1812.

Sam Houston lived long enough to oppose the secession of eleven southern states in 1861, as did a majority of the citizens of East Tennessee where he grew up. Middle and West Tennessee were strongly for secession. Tennessee furnished more men to Confederate armies than did any other state, except North Carolina and Virginia. Tennessee also provided more soldiers for the Union cause than did any other state that seceded. Great battles were fought at Fort Donelson (Fig. 8.8), Shiloh (Fig. 8.9), Stones River (Fig. 8.10), Chattanooga (Figs. 8.11 and 8.12), Franklin (Fig. 8.14), and Nashville (Fig. 8.15). One of the heroes of the Civil War was Sam Davis (Fig. 8.13), a young Confederate scout from Smyrna who was captured by Federal soldiers in Union-controlled territory. At the time, Davis had in his possession a number of papers giving information on Federal strength in Middle Tennessee. A Federal officer offered to pardon him if he would tell who gave him the information. Young Davis refused and went to his death on the gallows at Pulaski, preferring to die rather than to betray a friend. Other Tennesseans to gain fame were Confederate Gen. Nathan Bedford Forrest, "the wizard of the saddle," and Adm. David G. Farragut, U.S.Navy, Tennessee's greatest naval hero and the first full admiral in the U.S. Navy. At the Battle of Mobile Bay, he gave his immortal words remembered as: "Damn the torpedoes, full speed ahead!"

Tennessee's best-known claim to fame in the Spanish-American War was that the gunboat *Nashville* fired the first shots of the war over the Spanish ship *Buena Ventura*. The American sailors boarded it and brought it seventeen miles into Key West, Florida. In this war, more Tennesseans volunteered to fight than could be accepted.

During World War I, 78,825 Tennesseans were in some branch of the armed services. Our state ranked fifth in the number of Congressional Medals of Honor awarded. One Tennessean to win it was Sergeant Alvin York, Tennessee's and America's greatest World War I hero. On October 8, 1918, he single-handedly killed twenty Germans and forced 132 more to surrender. Marshall Ferdinand Foch called York's deed "the greatest thing accomplished by any private soldier of all the armies of Europe."

During World War II, another distinguished Tennessean made his mark. Cordell Hull, President Roosevelt's secretary of state from 1933 until 1944, was a leading statesman and diplomat of the war. Three hundred thousand Tennesseans served in the various military branches during World War II, and tremendous preparatory activities took place. Among the state's military facilities were the Air Classification Center in Nashville, a balloon barrage center in Henry County (Fig. 8.22), Camp Campbell near Clarksville (Fig. 8.19), Camp Forrest at Tullahoma (Figs. 8.20 and 8.21), Smyrna Army Air Field (Fig. 8.26), the Naval Air Technical Training Center in Memphis (Fig. 8.24), a naval air base in Millington, a shell-loading plant near Milan, and a TNT plant near Chattanooga. Oak Ridge (Fig. 8.25) produced an atomic bomb, and for the 1944 invasion of Europe, extensive military maneuvers took place on Tennessee soil (Fig. 8.23).

Fig. 8.1. Boone's Falls, where Daniel Boone saved himself in an Indian battle near Johnson City.

Fig. 8.2. Fort Nashborough, Nashville.

132

Fig. 8.3. Corner of Gay and Main Streets,
1793, Knoxville.

Fig. 8.4. Block House at Old Fort near
Cleveland.

Fig. 8.5. The original Hermitage near Nashville.

Fig. 8.6. *David Crockett Cabin, Rutherford.*

Fig. 8.7. *David Crockett Courthouse and Mexican War Veteran Monument, Lawrenceburg.*

Fig. 8.8. *Fort Donelson, Dover.*

Fig. 8.9. Bloody Pond, Shiloh.

Fig. 8.10. Stones River Battlefield forts, Murfreesboro.

Fig. 8.11. Missionary Ridge, Chattanooga.

135

Gen. Thomas and Staff
on Lookout Mountain,
1863, Chattanooga, Tenn.
(From a War
Time Photograph.)

GEN.
KILPATRICK GEN.
THOMAS GEN.
WILLIAMS ? GEN.
BRANNAN ? ? GEN.
WHIPPLE KELLY LT.
KELLOGG

LOOKOUT MOUNTAIN

Fig. 8.12. Lookout Mountain, 1863,
Chattanooga.

Born near Smyrna, Tenn., Oct. 6, 1842.
Executed at Pulaski, Tenn., Nov. 27, 1863.

"If I had a thousand lives I would lose them all
here before I would betray my friends or the confidence
of my informer."

SAM DAVIS

Fig. 8.13. Confederate hero Sam Davis,
Smyrna.

Fig. 8.14. Confederate veterans at 1910 reunion
pictured in front of bullet-riddled smokehouse on
the grounds of the Carter House, Franklin.

136

Fig. 8.15. Old Fort Negley, Nashville.

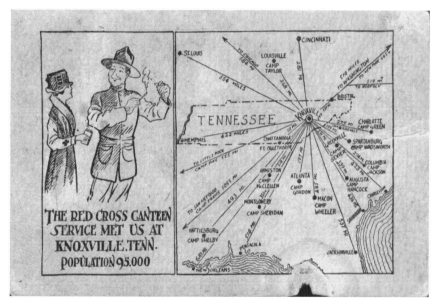

Fig. 8.16. Knoxville, 1918.

Fig. 8.17. Methodist Church, Pall Mall.

FIRST REGIMENT BAND, MEMPHIS, TENN.

MOBILIZATION CAMP, NATIONAL GUARD OF TENNESSEE—TENNESSEE STATE FAIR GROUNDS—NASHVILLE

Fig. 8.18. First Regiment Band, Memphis.

Enlisted Men's Barracks and Mess Halls, Camp Campbell, Ky.–Tenn.

Fig. 8.19. Camp Campbell near Clarksville.

AIR VIEW, CAMP FORREST, TENN.   3410

TULLAHOMA

HOSPITAL AREA

OLD CAMP PEAY AIRPORT

CAMP HD QT

PARADE GROUND

Photo by Hilliard Wood

Fig. 8.20. Camp Forrest, Tullahoma.

Fig. 8.21. Entrance to Camp Forrest,
Tullahoma.

Fig. 8.22. Camp Tyson.

Fig. 8.23. Pontoon Bridge across
Cumberland River.

Fig. 8.24. Naval Air Technical Training Center, Memphis.

Fig. 8.25. Oak Ridge.

Fig. 8.26. Hamburger Heaven, Smyrna Army Air Field, Smyrna.

*P*arks and Recreation

In 1926, Congress passed a bill to create the Great Smoky Mountains National Park. Land for the park, which was dedicated in 1940 by Franklin Roosevelt (Fig. 9.15), was donated by North Carolina and Tennessee. Knoxville has traditionally been the major gateway to the park that is bisected by the Newfound Gap Highway. The 1930s postcard view of the highway (Fig. 9.14) indicates it was then a gravel road. Gatlinburg, with more tourist courts and cabins than any of the other neighboring towns, became the most popular place to spend the night.

At the other end of the state, Reelfoot Lake (Figs. 9.35, 9.36, and 9.40) has long been acclaimed as a fisherman's paradise. Formed by a series of earthquakes in 1811 and 1812, this natural fish nursery is a popular state park that once encompassed twenty thousand acres of water. Between Reelfoot and the Great Smoky Mountains, there are dozens of other state parks. Postcard views of a number of them are included in this section.

I particularly enjoy the postcard views of early swimming pools. As a boy, I often went by automobile to swimming parties at Willow Plunge in Franklin (Fig. 9.13) and at Horn's Springs Resort in Wilson County (Fig. 9.22). Nashvillians who grew up before World War II often went to Horn's Springs Resort on the Tennessee Central Railroad and to Willow Plunge on the Franklin Interurban Railroad. My recollections of Willow Plunge are of a how cold the water was, of a knothole through which boys could look into the girls' dressing room, and of National Life and Accident Insurance Company picnics there during the 1960s. The postcard scenes of Whittle Springs Bathing Pool in Knoxville (Fig. 9.20) and the municipal swimming pool in Memphis (Fig. 9.26) are impressive. The Nolensville Pike Swimming Lake in Nashville (Fig. 9.33) was less so. Later, a more modern Cascade Plunge pool was built in Nashville.

On weekend afternoons in the fall, Tennesseans have enthusiastically attended high school and college football games. Traditionally, Municipal Stadium in Bristol (Fig. 9.3) was where Tennessee High and Virginia High determined which state would have bragging rights for the next year. The teams now play in Municipal Stadium every other year.

I remember watching Bill Wade lead Vanderbilt to a fourth-quarter victory over Ole Miss at E. H. Crump Stadium (Fig. 9.25) in 1951. Because my high school team played Memphis Central the night before, we were invited to sit on the Vanderbilt bench. In the Schools section of this book, there is a postcard of Shields Watkins Stadium (Fig. 14.28) as it appeared in the 1930s.

Fairs, such as the Bedford County Fair (Fig. 9.39) and the Clay County Fair were popular during the first half of the twentieth century. During the 1920s, Middle Tennessee children could see a life-size dairy cow made of pure creamery butter exhibited by the Tennessee cooperative creameries at the Tennessee State Fair. The postcard of the state fair (Fig. 9.34) shows a harness race in the foreground with the woman's building and grandstand in the background.

During the summers, Tennesseans have traditionally enjoyed hiking at various state parks, picnicking at our many lakes and waterfalls, and eating supper followed by dancing at resorts, such as at Rhea Springs (Fig. 10.31).

On weekends before World War I, a band from Guthrie, Kentucky, provided music for Saturday-night dances at Dunbar's Cave near Clarksville (Fig. 9.5). In a later generation, Roy Acuff and his "Smoky Mountain Boys" played there on weekends.

Jackson's Lancaster Park (Fig. 9.17), Knoxville's Chilhowee Park (Fig. 9.19), Memphis's Overton Park (Figs. 9.27 and 9.28), and Nashville's Centennial Park (Fig. 9.30) were among the state's premier municipal parks during the first half of the twentieth century. These parks and others, such as Knoxville's Fountain City Park and Nashville's Glendale Park (Fig. 9.31), were easily accessible by electric trolley lines. In Knoxville, you could reach either park on cars operated by the Knoxville Railway & Light Company. Glendale Park closed during the depression, a victim of hard economic times and the popularity of automobiles. Greenwood Park (Fig. 9.32), the first park to serve Nashville's black community, included a ball park, swimming pool, amusements, and picnic facilities. It remained open until 1949.

Chattanooga's Incline Railway up Lookout Mountain (Fig. 9.8) was extremely popular when the postcard view of it in this section was published in about 1918.

The 4,750-foot-long incline was, and may still be, the steepest in the world.

Some children were fortunate enough to attend summer camps. Among those in Tennessee were Camp Nakánawa at Mayland (Fig. 9.24) and Camp Riva-Lake at Winchester, both for girls, and Camp Elklore at Winchester for boys. Other children spent happy summer days at Ovoca near Tullahoma, where my grandfather was camp physician, or at the Monteagle Sunday School Assembly. While children were being well entertained at the assembly's playground (Fig. 9.29), their fathers would often play golf on the University of the South golf course (Fig. 9.38) five miles away. The Sewanee course was renowned for its sand greens, but better courses were found in our major cities, such as at the Country Club of Memphis or the Chattanooga Golf and Country Club (Fig. 9.2).

During the winter season, Chattanooga couples who liked movies particularly enjoyed going to the Bijou Theatre. In Bristol, the Fairyland Theatre was popular. Before World War I, Hopkins' Grand Opera House in Memphis was one of the state's most fashionable theaters.

Fig. 9.1. Great Stone Door, Beersheba Springs.

Fig. 9.2. Chattanooga Golf and Country Club, Chattanooga.

Fig. 9.3. Municipal Stadium, Bristol.

Fig. 9.4. Engel Stadium, Chattanooga.

Fig. 9.5. Dunbar's Cave, Clarksville.

143

Fig. 9.6. Ocoee River, home of the 1996 Summer Olympics canoe/kayak whitewater slalom competition near Cleveland.

Fig. 9.7. Fall Creek Falls State Park.

Fig. 9.8. Incline Railway up Lookout Mountain, Chattanooga.

Fig. 9.9. Cane Creek Falls in Fall Creek Falls State Park.

Fig. 9.10. Mt. Le Conte above Gatlinburg.

Fig. 9.11. Ozone Falls, Ozone.

CUMBERLAND GAP, TENN.

Fig. 9.12. Cumberland Gap.

Willow Plunge Swimming Pool, Franklin, Tenn.

Fig. 9.13. Willow Plunge Swimming Pool,
Franklin.

770 NEW FOUND GAP HIGHWAY, NEAR GATLINBURG, TENN. IN THE GREAT SMOKY MOUNTAINS NATIONAL PARK

Fig. 9.14. Newfound Gap Highway
near Gatlinburg.

146

Fig. 9.15. Dedication of Great Smoky
Mountains National Park.

Fig. 9.16. Sagamore Lodge, Chickasaw
State Park near Henderson.

Fig. 9.17. Lancaster Park, Jackson.

The old swimming hole and lodge at Pickett State Park, Jamestown, Tennessee.

Fig. 9.18. Pickett State Park, Jamestown.

BRIDGE, LAKE AND FINE ARTS BUILDING.

CHILHOWEE PARK, NATIONAL CONSERVATION EXPOSITION GROUNDS, KNOXVILLE, TENN.

Fig. 9.19. Chilhowee Park, Knoxville.

The Whittle Springs Bathing Pool, Knoxville, Tenn.—34

Fig. 9.20. Whittle Springs Bathing Pool, Knoxville.

148

Fig. 9.21. Spout Spring, Lawrenceburg.

Fig. 9.22. Horn's Springs Resort near Lebanon.

Fig. 9.23. Cub Creek Lake, Natchez Trace
State Park near Lexington.

149

THE WIGWAM, CAMP NAKÁNAWA, MAYLAND, TENNESSEE.

Fig. 9.24. The Wigwam, Camp Nakánawa, Mayland.

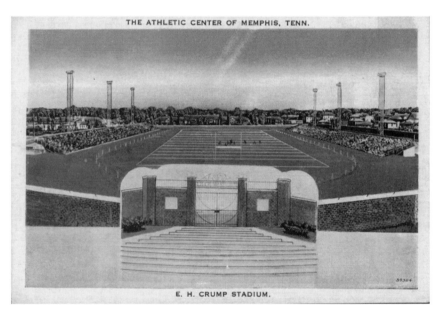

THE ATHLETIC CENTER OF MEMPHIS, TENN.

E. H. CRUMP STADIUM.

Fig. 9.25. E. H. Crump Stadium, Memphis.

MUNICIPAL SWIMMING POOL, MEMPHIS, TENN.

Fig. 9.26. Municipal Swimming Pool, Memphis.

Fig. 9.27. Overton Park, Memphis.

BEAR PIT AT ZOO, OVERTON PARK, MEMPHIS, TENN.

Fig. 9.28. Zoo, Overton Park, Memphis.

CHILDREN'S PLAYGROUNDS MONTEAGLE, TENN.

Fig. 9.29. Children's playgrounds, Monteagle
Sunday School Assembly, Monteagle.

151

Fig. 9.30. Centennial Park, Nashville.

Fig. 9.31. Glendale Park, Nashville.

Fig. 9.32. Greenwood Park, Nashville.

Fig. 9.33. Nolensville Pike Swimming Lake,
Nashville.

Fig. 9.34. Tennessee State Fairgrounds,
Nashville.

Fig. 9.35. Shaws Park, Reelfoot Lake.

Fig. 9.36. Spillway, Reelfoot Lake.

Fig. 9.37. Open Lake, Ripley.

OPEN LAKE NEAR RIPLEY, TENNESSEE

UNIVERSITY OF THE SOUTH GOLF COURSE

Fig. 9.38. University of the South Golf Course, Sewanee.

Meet me at the Bedford County Fair, Shelbyville, Tenn. Sept. 2, 3, & 4, 1909.

Fair Ground Shelbyville, Tenn.

Fig. 9.39. Bedford County Fair, Shelbyville.

REELFOOT LAKE AT TIPTONVILLE, TENN., IS THE NATION'S FINEST NATURAL FISH HATCHERY

Fig. 9.40. Reelfoot Lake, Tiptonville.

Railroad Park, Union City, Tenn.

Fig. 9.41. Railroad Park, Union City.

155

People

The first postcard in this section is of the Bristol, Tennessee, Fire Department Hose Company No. 2 (Fig. 10.1). In the early years of the twentieth century, a fireman was often judged by how long he could stay in a smoke-filled building with no protective breathing apparatus. Those who could stay the longest were called "smoke eaters." Probably, several of the volunteer fire-fighters in this hose company were "smoke-eaters."

The postcard of the Rathskeller on Cherry Street in Chattanooga (Fig. 10.3) reminds me of the first time I ate there in 1958. That night there was enough smoke in the dining room to make me think there might have been a fire. Of course, there was not, but there was plenty of beer and sauerkraut. That evening, a former Chattanooga Central football star, Bobby Hoppe, was present.

During the depression, nearly all the laborers mining phosphate for the Federal Chemical Company of Columbia (Fig. 10.4) were African Americans. The postcard shows them posed for their picture on payday. It also reveals how deeply strip mining scarred the land. In those years, state laws governing the reclaiming of land were much less restrictive than they are now.

The postcard of Edward Ward Carmack (Fig. 10.5) was published during the bitter prohibition fight in Tennessee. Carmack, an editor of the *Nashville Tennessean* and a former state senator, was killed on a downtown Nashville street in 1908 by Robin Cooper. A jury found Cooper and his father, Duncan Cooper, who was also present, guilty of second degree murder. Instantly, Carmack became a martyr of prohibition. Sometime later, Gov. Josiah Patterson pardoned both Coopers with the comment: "It took the Supreme Court seventy-two days to decide this case and it decided it wrong. It took me twenty-two minutes and I decided it the right way."

The two young ladies posed on Lookout Mountain's Umbrella Rock (Fig. 10.13) were duplicating poses made by thousands of tourists to Lookout Mountain over the years. As many as thirty people have stood upon the rock's flat surface at one time. It is possible that more postcards have been published of Umbrella Rock than of any other sight in Tennessee. Notice the whimsical names of the nine "East Tennessee Beauties" on the post-card published in 1906 (Fig. 10.6).

Providing a stark contrast to the East Tennessee beauties is the postcard view (Fig. 10.16) of a prison official standing outside a cell in the Tennessee State Penitentiary. The photograph probably dates to about 1907, ten years after the prison opened in West Nashville. The prison was described in 1921 as "modern in character and convenience."

The postcards of the Lynnville and Nashville base-ball teams show the pride of the players on both squads. The caliber of their play was somewhat dif-ferent, however. The Lynnville team (Fig. 10.17) competed against amateur teams in the Giles and Marshall County areas. Their picture was published by Rupert W. Waldrop, a Lynnville druggist. His son Frank C. Waldrop of Washington was one of Cissy Patterson's favorite editors at the *Washington Times-Herald*. The Nashville Volunteers (Fig. 10.24) were the 1908 Southern League champions. Grantland Rice called their championship game "the greatest game ever played in Dixie."

The unusual photograph of Dad Lively with five little girls (Fig. 10.19) was taken in McMinnville during a Red Cross parade. A less formal parade took place in Pulaski in about 1912 when Henry Ragsdale took his daughter Mary and eighteen of her friends for a ride in his new automobile (Fig. 10.28). Mary, who later married David R. Wade of Pulaski, was standing on the left running board.

The postcard photograph of W. C. Handy's band (Fig. 10.21) was taken in 1918. From Beale Street, W. C. Handy brought the "blues" to Memphis, twentieth-century America, and the world. A supporter of Memphis political titan E. H. "Boss" Crump, Handy's band played for Crump's mayoral campaign appearances in 1909. One of those tunes was later published as "The Memphis Blues." Notice the tribute to R. R. Church on the drum. Church was a preeminent black political and business leader. His father, R. R. Church Sr., a millionaire, was considered to be the most important black business and civic leader in Memphis between Reconstruction and World War I.

The postcard of Clarence Saunders's Piggly Wiggly (Fig. 10.20) was published in 1932, sixteen years after he launched his grocery business. Saunders revolutionized the American grocery industry by employing such innovative business methods as self-service, cash-and-carry, high-volume and low-profit margins. Saunders's Memphis mansion, nicknamed the "Pink Palace" by Memphians, is shown in figure 5.23.

The postcard picture of Roy Acuff and his Smoky Mountain Boys (Fig. 10.26) was taken on the stage of the Grand Ole Opry when Roy was barely thirty years old. To the extreme right is George D. Hay, "the solemn Old Judge." To the extreme left is Pete Kirby, whose stage name was "Brother Oswald." Pete played the steel guitar and sang tenor. The lady is Rachel Veach, the first and only woman ever to accompany that band. To her left is Lonnie "Pap" Wilson, who was both a comedian and a skillful guitar player.

When assembling the postcards for this section, I could not help but notice the contrast between the interesting picture of Ike Keele (Fig. 10.15), known around Manchester in the 1930s as "Old Black Joe," and the postcard of three prominent African-American physicians from Nashville (Fig. 10.27), who were also avid deer hunters. The two postcards of visitors to Reelfoot Lake (Figs. 10.29 and 10.30) speak to the continuity of the lake's popularity from generation to generation. The postcard of the two couples with their guide was postmarked 1912.

The last postcard I will comment on is the photograph of Winston Wiser sitting on champion Merry Go Boy (Fig. 10.34). In 1947 and 1948, Merry Go Boy won the world's Walking Horse Championship in Shelbyville, Tennessee, succeeding Midnight Sun, who had won in 1946.

Fig. 10.1. Hose Company No. 2, Bristol.

Fig. 10.2. Members of Pilgrim Church, Chattanooga.

Fig. 10.3. Rathskeller, Chattanooga.

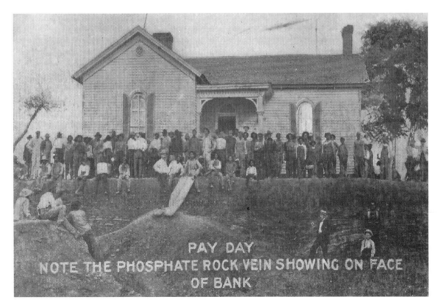

PAY DAY
NOTE THE PHOSPHATE ROCK VEIN SHOWING ON FACE
OF BANK

Fig. 10.4. Federal Chemical Company, Columbia.

Fig. 10.5. Edward W. Carmack, Columbia.

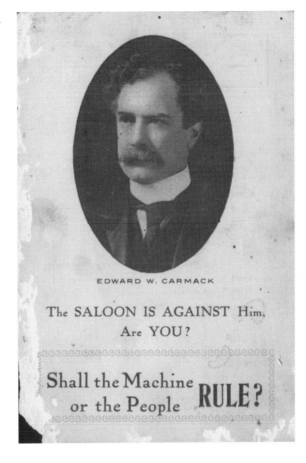

Fig. 10.5. Edward W. Carmack, Columbia.

Fig. 10.6. Young women from East Tennessee.

Fig. 10.7. Wiley Oakley in Great Smoky Mountains
National Park near Gatlinburg.

Fig. 10.8. Group picture, Gibson Wells.

Fig. 10.9. May Pole, Lancaster Park, Jackson.

Fig. 10.10. Kinzel Springs.

160

Fig. 10.11. The Walburn Clark Little Symphony, Farragut Hotel, circa 1925, Knoxville.

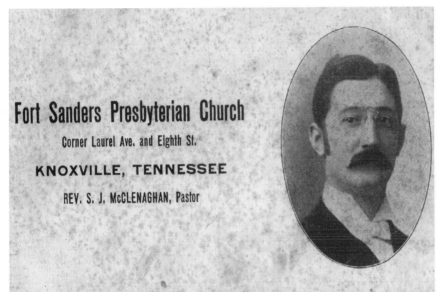

Fig. 10.12. Rev. S. J. McClenaghan, Knoxville.

Fig. 10.13. Umbrella Rock, Lookout Mountain.

Fig. 10.14. Fat Man's Squeeze, Rock City Gardens,
Lookout Mountain.

Fig. 10.15. Ike Keele, Manchester.

Fig. 10.16. Tennessee State Penitentiary,
east wing, Nashville.

162

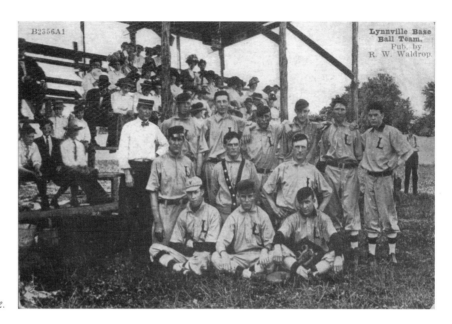

Fig. 10.17. Baseball team, Lynnville.

Part of the 95 Hall-Moody Students in State Institute, McKenzie, Tenn. We are—

Fig. 10.18. Hall-Moody students, McKenzie.

*Fig. 10.19. Dad Lively and friends,
McMinnville.*

Fig. 10.20. Interior of Clarence Saunders's Store, 1932, Memphis.

Fig. 10.21. W. C. Handy Band, 1918, Memphis.

Fig. 10.22. Harbin's Tourist Court, Memphis

CHILDREN'S PLAYGROUND, OVERTON PARK, MEMPHIS, TENN.

Fig. 10.23. Children's playground, Overton Park, Memphis.

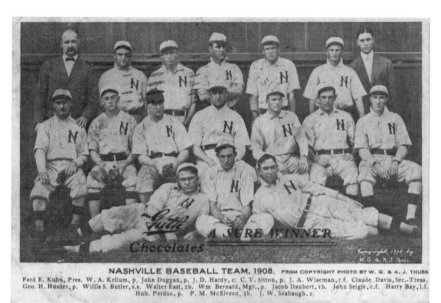

NASHVILLE BASEBALL TEAM, 1908. FROM COPYRIGHT PHOTO BY W. G. & A. J. THUSS

Ferd E. Kuhn, Pres. W. A. Kellum, p. John Duggan, p. J. D. Hardy, c. C. V. Sitton, p. J. A. Wiseman, r.f. Claude Davis, Sec.-Treas. Geo. H. Hunter, p. Willis S. Butler, s.s. Walter East, 2b. Wm Bernard, Mgr., p. Jacob Daubert, 1b. John Seigle, c.f. Harry Bay, l.f. Hub. Perdue, p. P. M. McElveen, 3b. J. W. Seabaugh, c.

Fig. 10.24. Nashville Vols baseball team, 1908, Nashville.

MEN'S GLEE CLUB   DAVID LIPSCOMB COLLEGE, NASHVILLE, TENN.   ROBERT G. NEIL, DIRECTOR

Fig. 10.25. Men's Glee Club, David Lipscomb College, Nashville.

165

N. B. C. BROADCAST OVER WSM WITH SOLEMN OLD JUDGE

Fig. 10.26. NBC broadcast over WSM with the Solemn Old Judge and Roy Acuff, Nashville.

Three members of the Nashville Sportsmans Club Inc. Nashville, Tenn. attend annual deer hunt in the state of Louisiana

WILBUR E. PANNELL, M. D., HENRY H. WALKER, M. D., MATTHEW WALKER, M. D.

Fig. 10.27. Sportsman's Club, Nashville.

General agents for Giles, Maury, Marshall, Lincoln, Moore, Lawrence Counties. The home of the famous Ford Motor Cars. Accessories, Supplies and Repairs. Pulaski, Tenn.

PHOTO BY APPLETON

Fig. 10.28. Birthday ride in Henry Ragsdale's automobile, Pulaski.

Fig. 10.29. Reelfoot Lake.

Fig. 10.30. Reelfoot Lake.

Fig. 10.31. Hotel Porch, Rhea Springs.

167

Fig. 10.32. Tennessee Valley Hand weavers, Rockwood.

Fig. 10.33. Early colonists, Rugby.

Fig. 10.34. Merry Go Boy, Tennessee Walking Horse National Celebration World Champion, Shelbyville.

Green No. 4, Golf Links, Tate Spring, Tenn.

Fig. 10.35. Green No. 4, Golf Links,
Tate Spring.

THE MINERAL WELL IN OLD COURT HOUSE YARD, TROY, TENN.

Fig. 10.36. The mineral well in Old Court
House Yard, Troy.

One of Union City's Popular Dance Bands
Union City, Tenn.

Fig. 10.37. One of Union City's popular
dance bands, Union City.

169

Private Buildings

Early in the twentieth century, small-town banks were sources of community pride. The Bank of Alexandria (Fig. 11.1) was in DeKalb County. Founded about 1815, Alexandria, Tennessee, was named after Alexandria, Virginia. The Tennessee town's population in 1890 was 900. One hundred years later it was 730. The Bank of Goodlettsville, identified in figure 11.11 as First National Bank, is gone, but the building, built in 1900, remains as a florist shop.

This is the second time I've published a postcard view of Bristol's "new YMCA Building" (Fig. 11.5). The last time I did so was in *The Volunteer State of the Y*, a YMCA newsletter that I edited during the 1980s. That time, a YMCA member in Bristol complained that YMCA members from elsewhere might think the building was new in 1985. It wasn't. It was new in 1912.

The Crook Sanitorium (Fig. 11.17) was run by a Jackson, Tennessee, family noted for its physicians. Two of them, Dr. William G. Crook of Jackson and Dr. Angus M. G. Crook of Nashville, are friends of mine. Jackson's eight-story First National Bank (Fig. 11.13) stood until recently on the north side of the public square. Built in 1924–1925, the First National Bank was demolished to make way for a new City Hall.

During the 1920s, the Memphis skyline changed materially. The twenty-nine-story Sterick Building (Fig. 11.24) became the newest, tallest, and largest of Memphis's office structures, relegating the twenty-one-story Columbian Mutual Tower (Fig. 11.23) to second place.

In Nashville, the first two high-rise office structures to be built were the First National Bank (Fig. 11.25) and the Stahlman Building (Fig. 11.26), constructed in 1905 and

1906, respectively. Now vacant, the First National Bank Building's name has changed three times. When this postcard was published, it was the Independent Life Building.

Cummins Station (Fig. 11.33) was the brainchild of L & N Railroad President Milton Smith. It was built in 1907 to entice wholesale companies near Nashville's riverfront to move to the new warehouse beside L & N's Union Station, thereby discouraging the Southern and the Illinois Central Railroads from acquiring the Tennessee Central. This short-haul line would suffer if its shippers deserted the wholesale district adjacent to their terminal. The idea worked perfectly. Notice the C. T. Cheek & Son sign on the side of Cummins Station. This wholesale grocery business, owned by Christopher T. Cheek and sons, Leslie and Will T., was one of the first firms that moved to Cummins Station. C. T.'s first cousin Joel Cheek also moved his company, Cheek Neal Coffee Company, there in 1907. His Maxwell House Coffee, named for a Nashville hotel, soon become famous for its slogan "Good to the Last Drop." In 1928, Joel Cheek sold his company to General Foods for $42 million.

Knoxville's first skyscraper was the ten-story Knoxville Banking and Trust Company Building (Fig. 11.21), usually called the Burwell Building, completed January 1, 1909. At the topping-out ceremony, ten thousand people gasped as a mule named Maude was hauled to the top by a crane. You can see the suspended mule in the postcard view of the structure. A year or so later, J. H. Bailey sent his wife in Hixon, Tennessee, a postcard of the building with the comment "This is the highest building in Knoxville. You can see how much we are ahead of Knox." He probably was referring to Chattanooga's new fifteen-story Hamilton National Bank Building (Fig. 11.2), constructed in 1910. Chattanooga's first skyscraper was the James Building (Fig. 11.6), completed in 1907.

The postcard of Eighth Street in Chattanooga (Fig. 11.7) shows the domed *Chattanooga Times* Building in the distance. Its publisher was Adolph S. Ochs, who bought the failing newspaper at age twenty with borrowed money. Within a decade he turned the *Times* into one of the most successful papers in the South. In 1896 at age thirty-eight, Ochs bought another failing newspaper—*The New York Times*. He transformed it into the best daily newspaper in the United States. Just as Joel Cheek capitalized on a catchy slogan, "Good to the Last Drop," Ochs coined the famous slogan, "All the news that's fit to print."

Early in this century, railroads established YMCAs at small towns along their lines. In 1880, the City of Cincinnati built a line from Cincinnati to Chattanooga. Originally called the Cincinnati Southern Railroad, it was leased to the Southern when the Oakdale YMCA postcard (Fig. 11.37) was published. The YMCA was built to accommodate railroad crews at Oakdale, a coal and crew-changing station in Morgan County.

This section includes two postcard views of opera houses. Staub's Opera House in Knoxville (Fig. 11.19) was built in 1871–1872 by a future Knoxville mayor, Peter Staub. By 1890, its name was changed to Staub's Theatre. As a boy, Adolph Ochs worked at Staub's Theatre as an usher. The less-known opera house in Paris, Tennessee, (Fig. 11.38) had a peculiar location. It was next door to J. R. Spicer's Funeral Home (Fig. 4.50).

Two of the more modern postcards shown in this section are of the bus station in Athens, Tennessee (Fig. 11.3), photographed in 1949, and the Booker T. Motel in Humboldt (Fig. 11.16), one of the few places where, during the last years of segregation, African Americans traveling between Nashville and Memphis on Highway 70A could find pleasant accommodations.

The postcard of Robinson's Drug Store (Fig. 11.8) in Dayton, Tennessee, would never have been published had not the idea been developed there to have a local high school science teacher, John Scopes, challenge the Tennessee law against teaching evolution by discussing the theory in his classroom. The drugstore pundits hoped that ensuing publicity might bring business to their town. It did!

Fig. 11.1. *Bank of Alexandria, Alexandria.*

Fig. 11.2. *Hamilton National Bank Building, Chattanooga.*

171

Fig. 11.3. Bus Station, Athens.

Fig. 11.4. Bank of Crockett, Bells.

Fig. 11.5. New YMCA Building, Bristol.

172

Fig. 11.6. James Building, Chattanooga.

Fig. 11.6. James Building, Chattanooga.

Fig. 11.7. *Eighth Street, showing* Chattanooga Times Building *in the distance, Chattanooga.*

Fig. 11.8. *Robinson's Drug Store, Dayton.*

Fig. 11.9. Mountain City Club, Chattanooga.

Fig. 11.10. Nashville, Chattanooga & St. Louis
Railway Station, Dresden.

Fig. 11.11. First National Bank, Goodlettsville.

Fig. 11.12. First Citizens National Bank, Dyersburg.

First Citizens National Bank Bldg., Dyersburg, Tenn.

FIRST NATIONAL BANK, JACKSON, TENN.——34

Fig. 11.13. First National Bank, Jackson.

Unaka and City
National Bank Bldg.,
Johnson City, Tenn.——23

Fig. 11.14. Unaka and City National Bank,
Johnson City.

175

M. & O. Station, Henderson, Tenn.   Pub. by Baird Drug Co.

Fig. 11.15. Mobile and Ohio Railway Station, Henderson.

Booker T. Motel, Humboldt, Tenn

Fig. 11.16. Booker T. Motel, Humboldt.

CROOK SANATORIUM, JACKSON, TENN.—23

Fig. 11.17. Crook Sanatorium, Jackson.

Fig. 11.18. First National Bank, Kingsport.

Fig. 11.19. Staub's Opera House, Knoxville.

Fig. 11.20. Southern Railway Depot, Knoxville.

Fig. 11.21. Knoxville Banking and Trust Company Building, Knoxville.

Fig. 11.22. Tennessee General Building, Knoxville.

Fig. 11.23. Columbian Mutual Tower, Memphis.

Fig. 11.24. Sterick Building, Memphis.

STERICK BUILDING, MEMPHIS, TENN.   6199.29

Independent Life Building,
Nashville, Tenn.

Fig. 11.25. Independent Life Building, Nashville.

Fig. 11.26. Stahlman Building, Nashville.   7420. The Stahlman Bldg., Nashville, Tenn.

Bank of Leipers Fork, Leipers Fork, Tenn.

Fig. 11.27. Bank of Leipers Fork, Leipers Fork.

*Fig. 11.28. Nashville, Chattanooga &
St. Louis & Illinois Central Depot,
Martin.*

N. C. & I. C. Depot, Martin, Tenn.   Photo by Byars.

Commercial Appeal Building,
Memphis, Tenn.

*Fig. 11.29. Commercial Appeal Building,
Memphis.*

J. GOLDSMITH & SONS CO. THE STORE OF BETTER VALUES, SERVING MEMPHIS SINCE 1870   100075

Fig. 11.30. J. Goldsmith & Sons Company, Memphis.

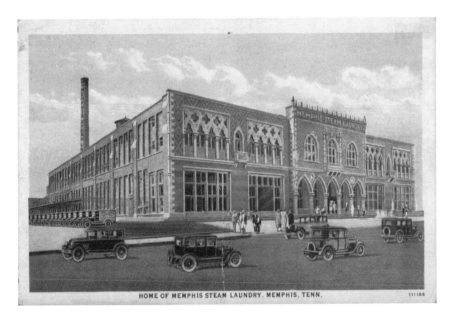

HOME OF MEMPHIS STEAM LAUNDRY, MEMPHIS, TENN.   111188

Fig. 11.31. Memphis Steam Laundry, Memphis.

New Depot, at Monteagle, Tenn.

Fig. 11.32. New Depot, Monteagle.

Fig. 11.33. Cummins Station, Nashville.

*Fig. 11.34. National Life and Accident
Insurance Company Building, Nashville.*

Fig. 11.35. Seventh Avenue Garage, Nashville.

Fig. 11.36. Union Station, Nashville.

Fig. 11.37. Railroad Department YMCA Building, Oakdale.

Fig. 11.38. Opera Block, Paris.

Opera Block, Paris, Tenn.

183

Picturesque Ridgetop.   5713

Fig. 11.39. L & N Railway Depot, Ridgetop.

"THE CLOCK" CAFE and SERVICE STATION HIGHWAY 45 SOUTH SELMER, TENN.

Fig. 11.40. "The Clock" Cafe and Service Station, Selmer.

L. & N. Passenger Depot, Springfield, Tenn.

Fig. 11.40. L & N Passenger Depot, Springfield.

Fig. 11.42. Cypress Point, Tiptonville.

Fig. 11.43. People's Bank, Smyrna.

Fig. 11.44. Blacksmith Shop, Tate Spring.

Public Buildings

From the date of its entry into the Union as the six-teenth state in 1796 until 1811, the state capital was Knoxville, except for one day when it was Kingston. After the capital became Nashville for several years, it changed again to Knoxville in 1817–1818. From then on, it would be in Middle Tennessee, first in Murfreesboro and later in Nashville, which was designated Tennessee's permanent capital in 1843. During the years the state capital was Knoxville, no capitol building was ever built by the State of Tennessee. The homes of John Sevier, our first governor, served as our Capitol during his terms of office. This practice continued under his successors, Achibald Roane and Willie Blount. The postcard of the "Old State Capitol" in Knoxville (Fig. 12.27) is of an early tavern where the legislature is thought to have met. Also included is a postcard of the State Capitol in Nashville (Fig. 12.37), erected between 1845 and 1853 at a cost of $2,500,000. Notice Clark Mills's equestrian statue of Andrew Jackson, erected in 1880 on the east grounds.

The Benton County Courthouse (Fig. 12.2) stood from 1917 until 1974. The Cannon County Courthouse at Woodbury (Fig. 12.44) was built in 1836 at a cost of $13,000. The building burned in 1934. The handsome Davidson County Courthouse (Fig. 12.36) was designed by W. F. Strickland, son of William Strickland, the architect for the State Capitol. This courthouse was torn down to make way for the present Davidson County Courthouse, built in 1937.

The Victorian Hamilton County Courthouse (Fig. 12.7) was built in 1879 at a cost of $100,325. It was destroyed by fire in 1910. During the 1950s, I met

Joe Richardson Sr., the genial Hamilton County Trustee. He was known for saying "hidy, hidy, hidy" to everyone he met in downtown Chattanooga because he was forgetful of names. Notice the twin horse-watering troughs in front of the handsome Knox County Courthouse (Fig. 12.25), erected in 1885. The Lincoln County Courthouse (Fig. 12.16) was built in 1873 at a cost of $29,579.30. It was torn down in 1971. The White County Courthouse (Fig. 12.40) was demolished in 1974. The oldest existing courthouses shown are the Jefferson County Courthouse (Fig. 12.12), built in 1845; the Roane County Courthouse (Fig. 12.23), built in 1853; and the Williamson County Courthouse (Fig. 12.17), built in 1859. Two of these, the ones in Jefferson and Williamson Counties, are still in use as courthouses.

The U.S. Post Offices shown range from an extremely early one in Dayton, Tennessee (Fig. 12.11), to the handsome one in Cookeville (Fig. 12.10). I particularly like the postcard of the Cleveland Post Office (Fig. 12.9), which was postmarked 1915.

Two municipal auditoriums are shown. The Soldiers and Sailors Memorial Auditorium in Chattanooga (Fig. 12.8) was erected as a lasting memorial to the heroes of World War I. It cost about one million dollars and its main auditorium was designed to seat 5,500. The Municipal Auditorium in Memphis (Fig. 12.30) was built for three million dollars. Its mammoth amphitheater seats 12,500.

This section includes aerial postcard views of two Veterans Administration hospitals. The Mountain Home VA Hospital (Fig. 12.34) was established in 1903 to house veterans of the Civil War and the

Spanish-American War. Later it served the same purpose for veterans of both world wars. Located on 450 acres, it once consisted of 89 buildings, including a laundry building, a fire department, churches, a theater, and a post office. During World War II, the Veterans' Administration Hospital (Fig. 12.35), five miles from Murfreesboro, comprised 602 acres and over fifty buildings.

The City Hall in Humboldt (Fig. 12.19), built in 1912, is now the West Tennessee Regional Art Center. It was established through the generosity of Nashville's Dr. and Mrs. Benjamin H. Caldwell, whose gifts of art constitute the heart of the museum's collection. Dr. Caldwell is a Humboldt native.

Knoxville's Lawson McGhee Library (Fig. 12.26), dedicated in 1917, was possible through a gift made by Col. and Mrs. Charles McGhee in memory of a daughter. The building, which houses the renowned McClung Collection, was torn down in 1975. Memphis's Cossitt Library (Fig. 12.31), which resembled a red sandstone castle, was located on the river bluff so visitors arriving by steamboat and rail could see it. It was built in 1893 in memory of Frederick H. Cossitt by his daughters. He was a northern businessman who made his fortune in Memphis.

During the 1930s and 1940s Tennessee had five major airports, two of which are shown in this section. During the late 1930s, the Memphis Municipal Airport (Fig. 12.33), completed in 1929, was served by three commercial carriers. The Tri-City Airport (Fig. 12.1) was dedicated November 5, 1937.

Fig. 12.1. Tri-City Airport, Bristol, Johnson City, Kingsport.

Fig. 12.2. Benton County Courthouse, Camden.

Fig. 12.3. Western State Hospital, Bolivar.

Fig. 12.4. Hickman County Jail, Centerville.

Fig. 12.5. Putnam County Courthouse, Cookeville.

Fig. 12.6. Carnegie Library, Chattanooga.

Fig. 12.7. Hamilton County Courthouse, Chattanooga.

Fig. 12.8. Interior, Soldiers and Sailors Memorial Auditorium, Chattanooga.

POST OFFICE, CLEVELAND, TENN,

Fig. 12.9. U.S. Post Office, Cleveland.

U.S. Post Office Cookeville, Tenn.   Z-212

Fig. 12.10. U.S. Post Office, Cookeville.

DAYTON, TENNESSEE FIRST POSTOFFICE

Fig. 12.11. Dayton's first post office.

190

JEFFERSON COUNTY COURT HOUSE, ERECTED IN 1845
DANDRIDGE, TENNESSEE

Fig. 12.12. Jefferson County Courthouse, erected in 1845, Dandridge.

4836   CITY HALL, NASHVILLE, TENN.

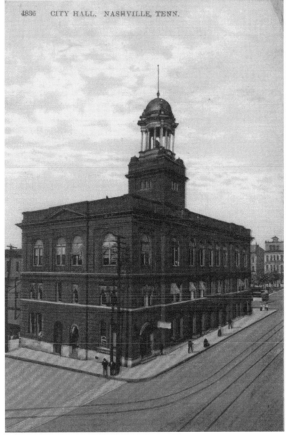

Fig. 12.13. City Hall, Nashville.

POST-OFFICE AND CUSTOM HOUSE, NASHVILLE, TENN.

*Dear Kathleen:— I recd your
card, was glad to hear you arrived
safe. will write soon*

KROPP. PUBL. MILWAUKEE. NO. 1295   *Love to all Lucile*

Fig. 12.14. Post Office and Custom House, Nashville.

191

Fig. 12.15. Decatur County Courthouse, Decaturville.

Fig. 12.16. Lincoln County Courthouse and Confederate Monument, Fayetteville.

Fig. 12.17. Williamson County Courthouse, Franklin.

Fig. 12.18. War Memorial Building, Gainesboro.

Fig. 12.19. City Hall, Humboldt.

Fig. 12.20. Carroll County Courthouse, Huntingdon.

193

Fig. 12.21. Court Square, Jackson.

Fig. 12.22. National Guard Armory, Jackson.

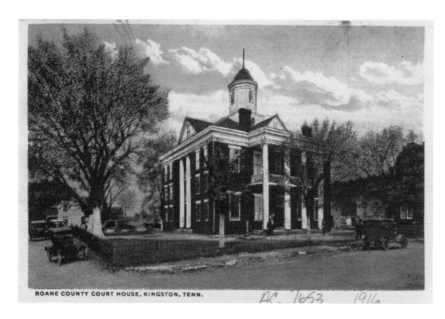

Fig. 12.23. Roane County Courthouse, Kingston.

194

Fig. 12.24. City Hall, Knoxville.

Fig. 12.25. Knox County Courthouse, Knoxville.

Fig. 12.26. Lawson McGhee Library, Knoxville.

Fig. 12.27. First State Capitol of Tennessee, Knoxville.

Fig. 12.28. Overton County Courthouse, Livingston.

Fig. 12.29. Coffee County Courthouse, Manchester.

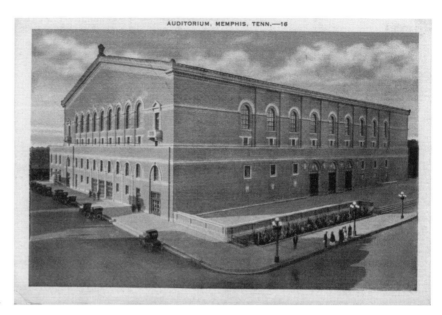

Fig. 12.30. Municipal Auditorium, Memphis.

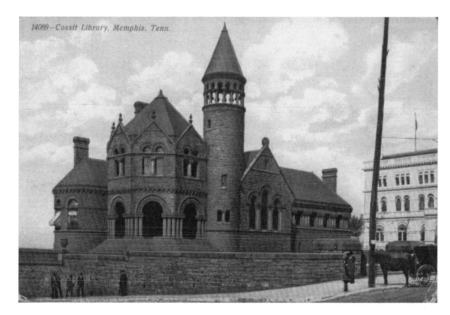

Fig. 12.31. Cossitt Library, Memphis.

Fig. 12.32. Custom House, Memphis.

Fig. 12.33. Municipal Airport, Memphis.

Fig. 12.34. Veterans Administration hospital
buildings, Mountain Home.

Fig. 12.35. Veterans Administration Hospital,
Murfreesboro.

*Fig. 12.36. Davidson County Courthouse,
Nashville.*

Fig. 12.37. State Capitol, Nashville.

*Fig. 12.38. Hardin County Courthouse,
Savannah.*

Fig. 12.39. DeKalb County Courthouse, Smithville.

Fig. 12.40. White County Courthouse, Sparta.

Fig. 12.41. United States Post Office, Union City.

Fig. 12.42. Morgan County Courthouse, Wartburg.

Fig. 12.43. Humphreys County Courthouse, Waverly.

Fig. 12.44. Cannon County Courthouse, Woodbury.

Rivers and Streams

Tennessee would not have been the sixteenth state to enter the Union had Richard Henderson and his Translyvania Company not bought from the Cherokees all the land between the Kentucky and Cumberland Rivers. He did so at Sycamore Shoals (Fig.13.65) on the Watauga River in 1775. Five years later, Capt. John Donelson led a party of men, women, and children on an epic 985-mile river voyage from Fort Patrick Henry on the Holston to Fort Nashborough on the Cumberland. The voyage was one of the greatest achievements in pioneer American history.

In Tennessee's earliest years, the Cumberland, Tennessee, and Mississippi Rivers were avenues that tied the Volunteer State, by flatboat and keelboat, to Natchez and New Orleans. Tennessee farmers were dependent on these markets to sell their produce. In December 1814, the Cumberland and Mississippi carried Gen. William Carroll's Tennessee troops to New Orleans to help Andrew Jackson win his great victory over the English.

The arrival of the steamboat *Andrew Jackson* in 1819 quickly elevated Nashville from a frontier outpost to a leading city in the southwest. The first steamboat to reach Knoxville was the *Atlas*, which arrived in 1828. The Tennessee River was, however, effectively broken into two sections by Muscle Shoals, a thirty-seven-mile stretch of white water with a drop of 134 feet. This natural barrier could be passed over by steamboats only during high water. Not until the completion of Wilson Dam at the lower end of Muscle Shoals in 1926 did the Tennessee River become truly navigable between Paducah and Knoxville.

When the Western District of Tennessee was opened for settlement following the Chickasaw Treaty of 1818, ferries were few and roads were poor and toilsome. Accordingly, many settlers from East Tennessee used the comparatively easier water route provided by the Tennessee to reach the Western District. Middle Tennesseans immigrating to West Tennessee often did so by floating down the Cumberland, the Ohio, and the Mississippi and then polling up the Hatchie, Forked Deer, or Obion. When the little steamboat *Rover* made its way up the narrow Hatchie to Brownsville's Landing in 1828, the villagers were ecstatic. A banquet was quickly prepared for the captain and his passengers. In 1852, state legislator Dr. Alexander Jackson received a letter from his wife, written from their home in Jackson, informing him that her Memphis grocer had written, saying that her groceries had arrived in Memphis and that he would send them up "as soon as the boats could run [the] Hatchie."

During the Civil War, Gen. U. S. Grant quickly realized that the Cumberland and Tennessee Rivers could provide access for his gunboats into the interior of Confederate territory and the very heart of the seceded states. With Grant's capture of Forts Henry and Donelson, it was inevitable that Nashville, the Confederacy's western arsenal, and the agricultural breadbasket surrounding the city would soon be under Federal control. A few months later, a Union fleet of ironclads on the Mississippi sank or disabled all but one of eight Confederate gunboats defending Memphis, and the city was immediately occupied.

In 1907, Clifton (Fig.13.60) was at the head of deep water navigation of the Tennessee River. A splendid line of packets, operated by the St. Louis & Tennessee River Packet Company, served the Wayne County town of twelve hundred that shipped crossties and lumber.

A new era in Tennessee came with the creation of the Tennessee Valley Authority in 1933. At that time, the Tennessee Valley was wasting. Seven million of its twenty-six million acres were suffering from erosion. In some counties, more than 50 percent of the families were on relief. The TVA's goal was to conserve the resources of the valley. It did so by building dams along the Tennessee River and tributaries to control floods, create electric power, deepen rivers for navigation, and provide recreational opportunities. Power from TVA dams would ultimately reach homes, factories, farms, and buildings in an area of approximately eighty thousand square miles.

Within the Cumberland River Basin there are ten lakes, created by the U. S. Army Corps of Engineers. These include the following lakes in Tennessee: Dale Hollow on the Obey River; Center Hill on the Caney Fork River; Cordell Hull, Old Hickory, Cheatham, and Barkley on the Cumberland; and J. Percy Priest on the Stones River.

The following postcards include several lakes and dams, such as Hale's Bar Dam (Fig.13.55), which in 1913 became the first combined navigation and power improvement dam on the Tennessee River. Even more postcards are of Tennessee streams, both large and small, taken before the ascendancy of hydroelectric power.

Fig. 13.1. Barren Fork River, McMinnville.

Fig. 13.2. Battle Creek, South Pittsburg.

Fig. 13.3. Bridge and dam, Caney Fork River, McMinnville.

Fig. 13.4. Center Hill Lake, Smithville.

Fig. 13.5. Norris Lake and dam, Clinch River.

Fig. 13.6. Looking up the Clinch River towards
the mouth of the Emory River between
Harriman and Kingston.

Fig. 13.7. Clinch River, Kingston.

Fig. 13.8. Cumberland River, showing the mouth
of the Obey River, Celina.

Fig. 13.9. Cordell Hull Memorial Bridge, Cumberland River, Carthage.

Fig. 13.10. Steamboat H. G. Hill on the Cumberland River.

Fig. 13.11. Cumberland River Bridge between Old Hickory and Madison.

206

SCENE ON THE CUMBERLAND, NASHVILLE, TENN.

Fig. 13.12. Wharf, Cumberland River,
Nashville.

Have seen things look this way here but not today. Will be home some day. 7-1-07 J.C.B.

CUMBERLAND RIVER STEAMER, PASSING THROUGH CLARKSVILLE, TENN.

Fig. 13.13. Steamboat on the Cumberland
River, Clarksville.

Cumberland River near Ft. Donelson, Dover, Tenn.

Fig. 13.14. Cumberland River, Dover.

207

Fig. 13.15. Doe River, Elizabethton.

Fig. 13.16. Duck River, Manchester.

Fig. 13.17. Duck River, Shelbyville.

208

Fig. 13.18. Stone bridge across Elk River, Fayetteville.

Fig. 13.19. Emory River, Harriman.

Fig. 13.20. Forked Deer River near Henderson.

209

Fig. 13.21. French Broad River.

Fig. 13.22. Douglas Dam, French Broad River.

Fig. 13.23. Boyd's Mill, West Harpeth River, Bingham.

Fig. 13.24. Hiwassee River, Cherokee National Forest, Reliance.

Fig. 13.25. South Holston Lake near Bristol.

Fig. 13.26. Holston River, Galbraith Springs.

211

Fig. 13.27. Cherokee Lake on Holston River.

Fig. 13.28. Little River near Knoxville.

Fig. 13.29. Excursion on Mississippi River, Dyersburg.

Fig. 13.30. Ferry Landing on the
Mississippi River, Tiptonville.

Fig. 13.31. Mississippi River at Confederate
Park, Memphis.

Fig. 13.32. Mississippi River Wharf, Memphis.

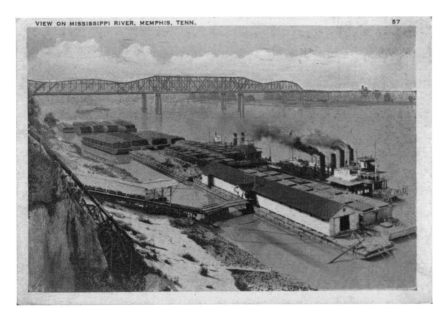

Fig. 13.33. Mississippi River, Memphis.

Fig. 13.34. Obey River, Riverton.

Fig. 13.35. Pigeon River, Newport.

Fig. 13.36. Piney River, Spring City.

A Piney River Scene, Pinewood, Tenn.

1318   HAND COLORED

Fig. 13.37. Piney River, Pinewood.

Fig. 13.38. Richland Creek, Giles County.

215

Fig. 13.39. Mill dam on Stones River,
Murfreesboro.

Fig. 13.40. Sulfur Fork Creek, Springfield.

Fig. 13.41. Old Ferry at the junction of the
French Broad and Holston Rivers, forming the
Tennessee River.

Fig. 13.42. Tellico River, Tellico Plains.

TELLICO RIVER CANYON, TELLICO PLAINS, TENN.

152—Chattanooga, Tenn.   Bluff View on Tennessee River.
One span of the bridge connecting Chattanooga and Hill City.

Fig. 13.43. Tennessee River, Chattanooga.

Brady's Lock and Dam, Tennessee River,
Thirty Three Miles below Chattanooga, Tenn.

*Fig. 13.44. Brady's Lock and Dam, Tennessee
River, thirty-three miles below Chattanooga.*

217

Island Home and Farm near Knoxville, Tenn.

Fig. 13.45. Tennessee River near Knoxville.

VIEW FROM THE OBSERVATION BUILDING - WATTS BAR DAM, TENNESSEE

Fig. 13.46. Watts Bar Dam, Tennessee River.

Air View of Chickamauga Dam, Tennessee River, Chattanooga, Tennessee   173

Fig. 13.47. Chickamauga Dam, Tennessee River, Chattanooga.

Fig. 13.48. *Sand barges on the Tennessee River,*
Knoxville.

Sand Barges at the foot of Central Street, Knoxville, Tenn.
Pub. by Monroe Howard Co.

Fig. 13.49. *Sunset on the Tennessee River.*

Two main types of dams comprise the TVA water control system which steps water productively, rather than destructively, down to the Tennessee River's mouth as shown in the above diagramatic map.

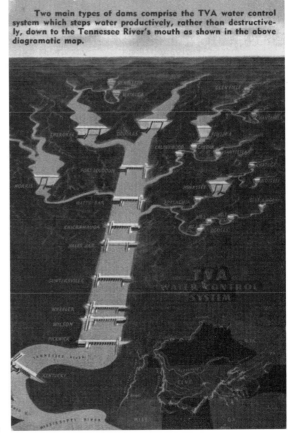

Fig. 13.50. *TVA Water Navigation System.*

Fig. 13.51. From the Chattanooga Golf and Country Club, Tennessee River, Chattanooga.

Fig. 13.52. Million Dollar Bridge over the Tennessee River, Chattanooga.

Fig. 13.53. Steamboat Chattanooga at the wharf, Tennessee River, Chattanooga.

Fig. 13.54. Moccasin Bend, Tennessee River, Chattanooga.

Fig. 13.55. Hale's Bar Dam, Tennessee River, Chattanooga.

Fig. 13.56. Rankin's Ferry, Tennessee River near Jasper.

Fig. 13.57. *Tennessee River, South Pittsburg.*

Fig. 13.58. *Pickwick Dam, Tennessee River.*

THE GOLDEN EAGLE
IN NAVIGATION LOCKS
PICKWICK DAM, TENN.

Pittsburg Landing, Shiloh National Military Park,
Pittsburg Landing, Tenn.

Fig. 13.59. *Pittsburg Landing.*

Fig. 13.60. Clifton Wharf, Tennessee River.

Fig. 13.61. Danville Elevator, Tennessee River.

Fig. 13.62. Eva Fishing Camp,
Kentucky Lake, Eva.

223

Fig. 13.63. U.S. 70 bridge over Kentucky Lake on the Tennessee River.

Fig. 13.64. Paris Landing State Park, Kentucky Lake.

Fig. 13.65. Sycamore Shoals, Watauga River.

Schools

Shortly after the Protestant Reformation, the Church of Scotland required that each church should have a schoolmaster and that all children, rich or poor, should be educated—the latter at the expense of the church. It was natural, therefore, that over two hundred years later, Presbyterian ministers should pioneer educational efforts on the Tennessee frontier, where so many settlers were of Scots-Irish descent. Among Tennessee's first schools were Martin Academy in Washington County (established about 1780), Davidson Academy near Nashville (established 1785), Greeneville College in Greeneville (chartered 1794), and Blount College in Knoxville (chartered 1794). The founding presidents of these schools were Samuel Doak, Thomas Craighead, Hezekiah Balch, and Samuel Carick, respectively, all Presbyterian ministers, and all but Carrick educated at the College of New Jersey, now Princeton University.

Despite the best efforts of preacher-teachers, Tennesseans were initially indifferent to education. After the Indian wars ended, interest gradually increased. Log cabins were built to be used both as schoolhouses and churches. Young men, often indifferently educated themselves, were employed as schoolmasters by nearby landowners.

In 1806, Congress appropriated large grants of land for state colleges. The next year, Blount College, near Knoxville, became a state institution known as East Tennessee College. Later, the school's name was changed to East Tennessee University, and finally, in 1879, to the University of Tennessee (Fig.14.16). Nevertheless, little thought was given early in the nineteenth century to public education. The prevailing idea was that education at public expense was for pauper children. Taxpayers, who generally sent their children to private schools, seminaries, and academies, were opposed to paying taxes for the education of children whose parents could not afford to send them to such schools.

In 1854, Gov. Andrew Johnson championed public education by advocating a tax to "give life and energy to our dying or dead system of common school education." After a bitter struggle in the legislature, his recommendations became law. Still, it would be 1873 before public schools became a reality. That year, legislation was passed providing for free schooling for children between six and eighteen. Secondary education received a boost in 1899 when county courts were given the power to establish high schools.

Higher public education was energized in 1875 when the legislature created a State Board of Education. Unfortunately, it provided no money to establish a normal school. That same year, Peabody Normal School opened in Nashville thanks to gifts by George Peabody, a northern philanthropist, and the availability of the campus of the University of Nashville, a successor school to Davidson Academy. Later, publicly funded normal schools were established at Johnson City (Fig.14.25), Murfreesboro (Fig.14.36), Clarksville (Fig.14.5), and Memphis (Fig.14.35). They evolved into today's East Tennessee State, Middle Tennessee State, and Austin Peay State Universities, and the University of Memphis.

After Reconstruction, private boys' schools sprang up like wildfire, particularly in Middle Tennessee. A smaller number of academies and women's colleges, such as the Columbia Institute in Columbia, Ward's Seminary in Nashville, and Soule College in Murfreesboro (Fig.14.37), provided limited opportunities for the education of women.

By 1905, there were at least twenty-four private boys' schools in Middle Tennessee. The most famous of these was Webb School in Bell Buckle (Fig.14.1). Its founder and longtime headmaster was the legendary W. R. "Sawney" Webb, one of the stalwarts in American secondary education. He taught his boys "to love excellence and to take pride in accuracy, without which all higher learning is limited and any genuine mastery impossible." During World War I, at least three private schools, Branham and Hughes in Spring Hill (Fig.14.51), Fitzgerald and Clarke in Tullahoma, and Castle Heights in Lebanon (Fig.14.29), were converted into military schools. By 1940, most of the state's private schools were gone because of fire, deaths of headmasters, the depression, or the emergence of stronger county school systems. Two West Tennessee boys' schools, McFerrin Training School in Martin and McTyeire Training School in McKenzie (Fig.14.32), as well as many Middle Tennessee boys' schools, were feeder schools for Vanderbilt University (Figs.14.42 and 14.43), founded in Nashville as a Methodist institution in 1875.

By 1900, Tennessee could boast of a number of denominational colleges and universities in addition to Vanderbilt. The list included Bethel College at McKenzie (Cumberland Presbyterian), Carson and Newman College (Fig.14.24) at Mossy Creek (Baptist), Christian Brothers College at Memphis (Catholic), Cumberland University (Fig.14.30) in Lebanon (Cumberland Presbyterian), Grant University at Athens and Chattanooga (Methodist), Greeneville and Tusculum College (Fig.14.17) at Tusculum (Presbyterian), Hiwassee College in Monroe County (Methodist), King College at Bristol (Presbyterian), Maryville College (Presbyterian), Milligan College (Christian), Nashville Bible School (Disciples), Southwestern Baptist University in Jackson (Fig.14.22), Southwestern Presbyterian University at Clarksville (Fig.14.6), the University of the South in Sewanee (Episcopalian) (Fig.14.49), and Washington College at Salem (Presbyterian).

At the turn of the century, Nashville and Jackson were centers for the education of African Americans. Fisk University (Fig.14.39), Central Tennessee College, and Roger Williams University were operating in Nashville, while Jackson's Lane College (Fig.14.21), chartered in 1895, grew to become one of the largest Negro colleges in the South, offering four-year college courses leading to bachelor of science and bachelor of art degrees. In 1909, Tennessee Agricultural and Industrial Institute (Fig.14.38) was established in Nashville, further adding to the city's black educational base. Knoxville also boasted of a black college in 1900. Knoxville College had been established there in 1875 by the United Presbyterian Church. At one time, Knoxville College was the black branch of the University of Tennessee.

Other colleges and universities, such as Martin College in Pulaski (Fig.14.46) and the University of Tennessee at Martin were junior colleges in their earlier years. Tennessee Tech in Cookeville (Fig.14.9) got its start in 1915 when the state legislature authorized funding for Tennessee Polytechnic Institute (then Dixie College).

SAWNEY HALL, WEBB SCHOOL, BELL BUCKLE, TENNESSEE

Fig. 14.1. Sawney Hall, Webb School, Bell Buckle.

The Brownsville Training School. Brownsville, Tenn.

Fig. 14.2. Brownsville Training School, Brownsville.

THE McCALLIE SCHOOL CAMPUS — CHATTANOOGA, TENNESSEE

Fig. 14.3. McCallie School, Chattanooga.

CAMPUS QUADRANGLE, UNIVERSITY OF CHATTANOOGA (LOOKING TOWARD MISSIONARY RIDGE), TENNESSEE.

Fig. 14.4. Campus Quadrangle, University of Chattanooga, Chattanooga.

227

Fig. 14.5. Girls' Dormitory, Austin Peay Normal School, Clarksville.

Fig. 14.6. Southwestern Presbyterian University, Clarksville.

Fig. 14.7. Centenary College, Cleveland.

228

Fig. 14.8. Columbia Military Academy, Columbia.

STUDENTS AND GROUNDS OF COLUMBIA MILITARY ACADEMY, COLUMBIA, TENN.

Fig. 14.9. Women's basketball team, 1920, Tennessee Technological University, Cookeville.

Fig. 14.10. Covington City School, Covington.

229

RHEA HIGH SCHOOL, DAYTON, TENN. *William J. Bryan debated on Darwinism* BT-1035

Fig. 14.11. Rhea High School, Dayton.

Distillery.

New School Bldg.

Old School.

Progress of Education in Lincoln Co., since Prohibition in Tennessee. Buildings located within one-half mile, Fayetteville, Tenn.

Fig. 14.12. Lincoln County buildings, Fayetteville.

Grover Hall, Grand View Normal Institute, Grand View, Tenn.

Fig. 14.13. Grover Hall, Grand View Normal Institute, Grand View.

Fig. 14.14. Battle Ground Academy, Franklin.

Fig. 14.15. Administration Building, Freed-Hardeman College, Henderson.

Fig. 14.16. Science Hall, University of Tennessee, Knoxville.

McCORMICK HALL, TUSCULUM COLLEGE, GREENEVILLE, TENN.

Fig. 14.17. McCormick Hall, Tusculum College, Greeneville.

PUBLISHED BY BRASFIELDS DRUG STORE.   PHOTO BY MRS. POWELL

PUBLIC SCHOOL, GREENFIELD, TENN.

Fig. 14.18. Public school, Greenfield.

Avery Hall,
Lincoln Memorial University,
Harrogate, Tenn.

Fig. 14.19. Avery Hall, Lincoln Memorial University, Harrogate.

Fig. 14.20. Lambuth College, Jackson.

Fig. 14.21. Lane College, Jackson.

Fig. 14.22 Southwestern Baptist University,
Jackson.

233

Fig. 14.23. Alvin C. York Institute, Jamestown.

Fig. 14.24. Carson and Newman College buildings, Jefferson City.

Fig. 14.25. Dormitory, East Tennessee State Normal School, Johnson City.

234

Fig. 14.26. High school, Jonesboro.

Fig. 14.27. High school, Knoxville.

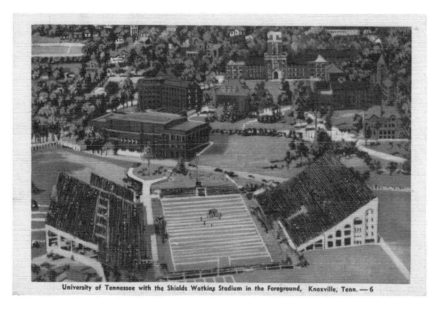

Fig. 14.28. Shields Watkins Stadium,
University of Tennessee, Knoxville.

235

Fig. 14.29. Castle Heights Military Academy, Lebanon.

Fig. 14.30. Caruthers Hall, Cumberland University, Lebanon.

Fig. 14.31. Fayette County High School, Somerville.

Fig. 14.32. McTyeire Training School, McKenzie.

Fig. 14.33. Various schools, Memphis.

Fig. 14.34. Southwestern College, Memphis.

237

ACADEMIC BUILDING, WEST TENNESSEE STATE NORMAL SCHOOL, MEMPHIS, TENNESSEE   72003

Fig. 14.35. Academic Building, West Tennessee State Normal School, Memphis.

MIDDLE TENNESSEE STATE TEACHERS COLLEGE, MURFREESBORO.   105151

Fig. 14.36. Middle Tennessee State Teachers College, Murfreesboro.

Soule College, Murfreesboro, Tenn.

Fig. 14.37. Soule College, Murfreesboro.

Fig. 14.38. Tennessee Agricultural and Industrial State College, Nashville.

Fig. 14.39. Jubilee Singers, Fisk University, Nashville.

Fig. 14.40. Hume-Fogg High School, Nashville.

Fig. 14.41. President Theodore Roosevelt at the University of Nashville, October 22, 1907.

LINE UP OF VANDERBILT FOOTBALL TEAM OF 1906

Fig. 14.42. Football team, 1906, Vanderbilt University, Nashville.

School of Medicine and Hospital, Vanderbilt University, Nashville, Tenn.—51

Photo by 165th Photo Section Air Corps, Tenn. Nat. Guard, Nashville.

Fig. 14.43. School of Medicine and Hospital, Vanderbilt University, Nashville.

240

Fig. 14.44. Ward-Belmont, Nashville.

A BIT OF THE PARK, WARD-BELMONT, NASHVILLE, TENN.

E. W. GROVE HENRY COUNTY HIGH SCHOOL, PARIS, TENN.

Fig. 14.45. E. W. Grove Henry County High School, Paris.

Fig. 14.46. Martin College women, Pulaski.

LAUDERDALE COUNTY HIGH SCHOOL. RIPLEY, TENN.

Fig. 14.47. Lauderdale County High School, Ripley.

Main Building Ruskin Cave College
Entrance Big Cave

Ruskin, Tenn.

Flashlight Interior Big Cave
Banquet Ruskin Cave College Students

Fig. 14.48. Ruskin Cave College, Ruskin.

3297 FORENSIC HALL, UNIVERSITY OF THE SOUTH, SEWANEE. TENN.

Fig. 14.49. Forensic Hall, University of the South, Sewanee.

242

Fig. 14.50. Baylor School, view from Signal Mountain.

WILLIS COURTS, BRANHAM & HUGHES SCHOOL, SPRING HILL, MAURY CO., TENN.

Fig. 14.51. Willis Courts, Branham and Hughes School, Spring Hill.

Fig. 14.52. James K. Shook School, Tracy City.

243

Index

Page numbers in boldface indicate postcard captions.

246